REVISED EDITION

The Maquis Connection

D1319464

GEORGE A KARP, MD

ISBN 978-1-944248-25-3

The first edition of *The Maquis Connection to Freedom* was written in 1984 by George Karp as a memoir of his life. This second new edition, released in 2015, focuses primarily on George and Gisy Karp's escape from Nazi Europe. This edition has been reorganized and edited to be concise while preserving the original author's voice and intent. We have added three new chapters and broadened the historic context from a variety of sources. We have also added photographs from our personal collections as well as historic archives.

This second edition is dedicated to Sharon Karp and supplements her excellent film, *A Song for You*, about which more information can be found at asongforyoumovie.com. We would like to thank Silvia Malagrino, who co-directed the film with Sharon. We also thank Shira Handler, Angela Koenig and Carol Karton for their edits and improvements to the text, and Nicole Ferentz for the graphic design.

—*Susan Bernstein and Larry Bernstein*

TABLE OF CONTENTS

A SONG FOR YOU

A FILM BY SHARON KARP
CO-DIRECTED BY SILVIA MALAGRINO

GEORGE AND GISELA KARP AND THEIR INFANT DAUGHTER ESCAPED THE NAZIS
CROSSING THE PYRENEES WITH THE HELP OF THE FRENCH RESISTANCE.
THE FILM REVEALS THE IMPACT OF THE HOLOCAUST ON THE NEXT GENERATION
AND CELEBRATES THE BRAVERY OF THOSE WHO RISKED THEIR OWN LIVES
TO SAVE THE FAMILY.

DIRECTOR, EDITOR, CINEMATOGRAPHY, ORIGINAL MUSIC **SHARON KARP**   CO-DIRECTOR, MOTION GRAPHICS, CINEMATOGRAPHY **SILVIA MALAGRINO**

I always knew that I would make a film about my family's escape from the Nazis: "running by night, hiding by day" across the Pyrenees from France to Spain, my mother wearing only high-heeled shoes, my sister Susie knowing she couldn't cry from hunger or fear, my father so tired he wanted them to go on without him. It was a story my mother told over and over—their monumental accomplishment, crossing to freedom with the help of the Maquis, the French Resistance. After my parents' deaths, I felt compelled finally to begin making a very personal film about their escape. During this process, I was forced to confront my own trauma as a child of survivors. My film, *A Song for You*, is a story of survival through strength of will, luck, and the help of others.

Sharon Karp filming Gisy Karp for A Song for You.

The film has brought a renewed interest in my father's book, a primary source I used in *A Song for You*. In the book, he recounts his life before and after the Anschluss, how he and my mother and sister escaped the Holocaust, and finally how they found safety in the United States.

The film and the book are interconnected, yet independent. They offer different insights into the same events, but they tell one story of survival.

All of the stories form a collective memory, a history of what happened to the few, the lucky ones who survived the Holocaust.

*A Prince
is Born
in 1902*

My story begins in 1902, the year I was born a prince. Please do not to take this statement literally. I use the term *prince*, not to signify birth privilege or aristocratic distinction, but rather to capture the subjective feeling that I had been treated as well, or perhaps even better than, a royal son.

My parents Eva and Ludwig Karp.

I cannot fully explain my good fortune, except to say that I was an only child, a latecomer, born ten years after my parents' marriage, and as such, I was spoiled and greatly loved by my mother and father.

Both of my parents were born in what is now Romania, and my grandparents were also born in the same general region. My father Ludwig was a custom tailor. He owned a very small business but was well-known for his low prices and expert workmanship. Because he could not afford to keep cloth in his store, his customers acquired fabric from other vendors and brought it to his shop. Depending on the volume of work, he might have three or four younger tailors working for him, but when times were hard, as they often were, he had to sew, press, and deliver everything himself.

We lived in a three-room house that was both my father's store and our residence. The entire shop consisted of one table for cutting and pressing, one leg-operated sewing machine, and two chairs.

My family was poor, like a typical Eastern European Jewish family portrayed in the stories of Shalom Aleichem, as depicted in *Fiddler on the Roof*. Still, this early period of my life was tranquil and cheerful.

Our meals at home were usually simple, but we were never hungry. Each week, my mother bought a half-kilo of expensive kosher meat for the Sabbath dinner. On weekdays we ate starchy meals, such as potatoes or noodles. For breakfast, my mother served us a cup of coffee and some bread without butter. Chicken was a treat and duck or goose was reserved for very special occasions. We did not celebrate birthdays or anniversaries, nor did any of our friends.

Eva, George, and Ludwig.

There were good times and bad times, but the approach of winter was always menacing. My father had to take on extra work to make money for firewood to heat the furnace and stove. The wood was kept neatly stacked in the courtyard next to the outhouse, and over the course of the winter, my father would cut the logs into pieces to fit into our stove.

My father was a quiet man of many interests and very rational. I would call him a pragmatist. He was also religious and attended synagogue regularly. We kept a kosher home and adhered to traditional Jewish customs, but early in my life, I became aware that this was not to be taken too strictly. Usually on Saturdays and holidays, no work was done in our little shop, but if the need for money was urgent, exceptions were made. Nevertheless, on those occasions, the prayers and formalities of the Sabbath were observed.

While not a scholar in the traditional Jewish sense, my father wore *tefillin* in daily morning prayers and held regular evening services at home, or when time was available, at the temple. For reasons never explained to me, I attended these ritual services only on Friday evenings and Saturday mornings.

My own feelings about religion were ambivalent. On one Yom Kippur during a break in the service, I sat on a park bench across the street from a pastry shop. I was shocked to see a very well-respected man who was the head of the congregation leave the shop eating a pastry in violation of the Day of Atonement fast. His behavior made an indelible impression on me and confirmed the hypocrisy of traditional religious customs and observance.

My father loved to read the daily newspaper and was knowledgeable about world events. He belonged to the local socialist organization, paying monthly membership dues and marching in the annual parade each May 1, which made me proud.

My mother, Eva, was a beautiful, simple, unassuming woman. Like many women of her time, she was poorly educated. She observed traditional Jewish customs but was not particularly religious. On High Holidays, she went with us to temple where services were led by our red-bearded, fire-and-brimstone Rabbi Ármin Horowitz. She sat upstairs with the other women who were partially hidden behind curtains. However, I knew my mother's customary place so I felt her presence. On Yom Kippur she fasted, remaining on her feet all day in order to attain more of God's mercy for her only son. She always told me how difficult this was, standing for hours in the unventilated sanctuary, countless candles burning which consumed much of the oxygen. Her prayers on this day were sufficient to give her comfort, satisfaction, and a good conscience for the remainder of the Jewish year.

George and Eva.

When I think of my mother, as I often do, I feel love and nostalgia, sorrow and shame, irreplaceable loss, and a void that can never be filled. She was devoted to her duties as a wife but without much love for her husband. All her love and ambition were for me, her son.

There were some who thought my mother spoiled me to the point where it would do me harm in the future. There is no doubt that her continuous flow of love brought me comfort and pleasure but it did have its drawbacks as well. I relied heavily on others and did not use my potential to its fullest.

My parents were fluent in Hungarian, Romanian and German, but with their Jewish friends they spoke Yiddish. In my youth, I was fortunate to learn three languages. My mother spoke to me in German, my father read me the newspaper in Hungarian, and we all conversed in Yiddish.

When I was six, my parents debated whether I should go to public school or to a Jewish school—*cheder*. My father's wish prevailed, and I entered *cheder* that year. My young, balding teacher terrified me when he walked into class with a stick in his hand. He screamed incessantly and hit the students to establish his authority. After a few days, I announced to my mother that I would not return. And that finished my Jewish education.

I entered a Hungarian public school with a wonderful library which was unusual for the time. By the first grade, I was reading fluently. Once a week, I would take home from the library four or five age-appropriate books to read. I remember my teacher's quizzical expression at this behavior as I was the only boy in the class of twenty who checked out a book.

I remember one incident, which occurred in my gymnastics class, of all places. We were playing in the schoolyard—a sandy, flat surface surrounded by an ugly metal fence. Our teacher ordered us to run toward the fence. He promised a prize to the child who was the fastest runner. I was a thin, light-footed boy but by no means an athlete. To my own surprise, I reached the fence first. The teacher was unhappy with the outcome, so he ordered us to repeat the competition. We all ran again, but because I was disappointed, or simply because I no longer had the stamina to run the second time, I did not make an effort to win, and I finished second to last.

At the time, the incident did not impress me, but years later I realized it had a great impact. As unlikely as it sounds, it was a traumatic event, depriving me of a competitive drive in later life.

The town where I grew up was called Nagyszeben, which was located in Transylvania and was part of the Austro-Hungarian Empire. I was born a subject of both the King of Hungary and the Austro-Hungarian Emperor. When I was a young man in Sibiu, I did not personally experience the anti-Semitism that was common in other parts of the Empire. The Austro-Hungarian Emperor tolerated the Jews and allowed them to prosper, albeit with some subtle pressure to convert to Catholicism. After the First World War, the Emperor abdicated and the Romanians invaded the town and renamed it Sibiu.

In my youth, the town had a population of 30,000 Germans, Slavs, Bulgarians, Croatians, Hungarians, Romanians, and Jews. Each group prayed in its respective church and spoke its own language, but all official communication was in German.

When I was a young man in Sibiu, I did not personally experience the anti-Semitism that was common in other parts of the Empire. The Austro-Hungarian Emperor

The city of Sibiu in front of the Carpathian mountains.

tolerated the Jews and allowed them to prosper, albeit with some subtle pressure
to convert to Catholicism.

The town of Sibiu is built on a hill next to the Cibin River, a small, slowly flowing
river with no fish. In the center of town, the one, main, cobblestoned street mounts
steeply, with a narrow walk for pedestrians, and three, intertwining, stone stairways.
Each day, the townspeople walked the wide, worn-out stairs to conduct their business.
In Sibiu, there are no major intersections. The streets are laid out the way the houses
were erected—at will, in all directions, with peculiar attics, and windows in the roofs
that look like eyes from a distance. This disorderly maze gives the town an unusual
charm. Today, Sibiu is recognized by the European Community as a historic landmark.

Sibiu's churches are located in the upper part of the city. The most impressive is the
Evangelical church with its high, slim, elegant tower that dominates the skyline. Also
in the upper part of the city are two squares: the larger *Grosser Ring* and the smaller
Kleiner Ring. When I was young, parades and big festivals were held at the larger square
along with military demonstrations and marches. I preferred the smaller square that
hosted a weekly market where peasants from the surrounding villages sold fruit, vegetables,
cheese, and homemade sausages from colorful tents. The smell of the sausages was
unbelievably tempting, but I could not eat them because I lacked the money, and
the sausages were not kosher.

Occasionally, a merry-go-round was erected, and laughing children rode in circles

The Evangelical Cathedral in Sibiu.

on wooden horses. One time I took part in this fun. I do not remember where I got the money, the few pennies needed for this, but I remember distinctly that I must have felt very guilty, for on my way home, I got my first migraine headache.

In Sibiu, movies were screened in large tents built on open grounds the way smaller circuses are built today. Children would sit rapt for hours on hard, wooden benches watching silent American westerns. A pianist would play loudly along with the film, and we would all root for the cowboys and boo the Indians.

Sibiu had a lovely theater where traveling groups performed operettas and dramas. In one performance of *Hamlet*, the ghost of Hamlet's father spoke in a ridiculous voice, and the audience, instead of being in awe, burst into a roar of laughter. It took time for the audience to recover and follow the dramatic events.

To my good fortune, this theater was located just five houses away from our residence. My mother liked to sing, and she knew all the popular melodies. She encouraged me to buy standing room tickets so I could watch the show from behind the last row of seats. It was unusual for a poor boy to go to the theater but I frequented as many performances as possible.

Sibiu also had a chamber music group, as well as an impressive and well-known symphony orchestra that performed monthly. My good friends Tibor Weiss and Erno Matyas used to take me to these various concerts. My friends had private lessons— Erno was an accomplished violinist—while I had the pleasure of simply listening. Of course, it would have been nice to study music as well, but my family could not afford lessons. I did not miss it at the time, just as I did not miss anything else that my friends had. For instance, my friends always had spending money and I never did, but it did not occur to me to feel different, to feel sorry for myself, or to be envious. Instead, I appreciated the new experiences, such as going to the theater to sit in Erno's family's season box. I should also mention the meals I shared with them. My exposure to fine food was as important to my cultural development as my education in classical music.

Grosser Ring in Sibiu.

Sibiu had other modern entertainments. One afternoon, with great anticipation, the entire town assembled on the outskirts of the village to view an incredible flying machine. After an interminable wait, the airplane appeared with the pilot distinctly visible. He was the famous Frenchman, Louis Blériot. He circled around and around in the sky until the show was over.

Inventions appeared in Sibiu decades later than in the great cities of the West. When I was a young man, the post office had the only telephone in town. Calls had to be arranged days in advance, but the quality was so poor that callers could rarely understand each other.

No one in town owned an automobile, but we were well served by a single streetcar that ran in both directions. Otherwise, to get around town, I walked. A horse and carriage were available only for the rich. The town lacked electricity. We used kerosene lamps at home, and the streets were dimly lit by gas lamps. We heard of air conditioning, but it was like a fairy tale. No one I knew had ever experienced it. Needless to say no television or phones interfered with our life. There was plenty of time to read, talk to parents and friends, and walk in the park or woods. By no means did we feel bored.

Sibiu street car.

To get away, we liked to visit a resort town, located about thirty minutes travel by coal-burning train. Visitors came to swim in the attractive salt lakes which were known for their healing properties. My parents and I liked to walk through the town and see the shops and restaurants. Those who could afford it stayed overnight in hotels, but when evening came, most of us took the slow train back to Sibiu.

Social customs in my youth were different from even a few decades later. Respectable women did not apply lipstick or powder their faces, only prostitutes did such things. Girls had to be chaperoned to a dance, wedding or any gathering.

When I was twelve, I discovered photography, which would become a lifelong passion. My mother's brother, my Uncle Mano, introduced me to the hobby. He was a professional photographer specializing in monochrome portraits, and he traveled internationally for his work as far as Cairo. We had many interesting conversations and I believed that he was my only relative who took a real interest in me. There were no camera shops in Sibiu, so I ordered some materials from a Budapest store's mail order catalogue. The equipment arrived with a small instruction manual and I immediately got to work.

My first camera was built on the principle of "camera obscura." It was a box camera with a simple small lens in front. To operate the camera, you opened the back of the box in the dark and placed horizontally, facing the lens, six small glass plates coated with light-sensitive emulsion material. The plates were held in place by a simple lever. When exposed, the plates could be manipulated by moving the lever. I was very fond of this camera. My friends and schoolmates admired my photographs. I worked hard to develop my skills and produced pictures that were quite good. I was proud to be the only student with such a device.

My only surviving photograph from my first camera is a single self-portrait. To make this photo, I instructed my mother to stand behind the camera, and open and close the shutter after a two-minute exposure. All this was done with natural light and a primitive, simple lens. In my later years I have worked with many fine cameras, but that first camera was by far my favorite.

My self-portrait with a camera obscura.

My Formative Years: 1918–1926

I was sixteen years old when World War I ended. The inflation and depression that devastated Europe after the war barely changed my family's standard of living. When you are poor, it is difficult to make a distinction.

After the war, the Austro-Hungarian Empire collapsed. Romanian troops marched into Hungary's Transylvania region and occupied it, and Sibiu's residents were advised to evacuate immediately.

In a panic, my mother and I left Sibiu, but my father stayed to manage the store. Our train left the station and traveled erroneously to the South, towards the invading Romanian army. I told my mother that we were traveling in the wrong direction, but she believed the train engineer knew where he was going. Only the next day was the mistake discovered and the train reversed course back to Hungary.

My Aunt Rebi with my cousin Lori, my mother and me.

We were welcomed in a little Hungarian town where the native peasant women offered steaming noodles to us poor refugees. Luckily, there was a small Jewish community in this town and I enrolled in the local school. We read in the newspapers that the Romanian army had fired cannon balls causing significant destruction to Sibiu. After a few months we returned home to Sibiu to find only minimal damage to the city's old fortification walls. My father recounted that it had been peaceful and safe in Sibiu, and that we could have stayed. Since then I have been very skeptical of the press.

My father told us that when the Hungarian army abandoned Sibiu, the soldiers changed to civilian clothes and hurried home, abandoning all of their equipment: weapons, uniforms, food supplies, ammunition, cannons, horses, and supply trucks. In turn, the townspeople carried off all they could. Surprisingly, no looting of private property took place. I suppose there was no need since all that was wanted could be picked up in the street.

From the ages of six to ten, I attended public grade school. After grade school, I passed a difficult baccalaureate exam to gain admission to the *gymnasium*, where I studied liberal arts for eight years. My classmates who failed the exam went to trade school for four years, followed by an apprenticeship. Graduates of the *gymnasium* could continue their studies at most European universities in their choice of fields such as medicine, law,

Jeno Pfeffermann, Mano Pfeffermann, and Erno Matyas.

engineering, or philosophy. University tuition was minimal but you had to pay for your own room and board.

The Sibiu *gymnasium* was closed after the Romanian invasion, so I attended a Hungarian parochial school in Fogaras. This small, backward city had no cultural institutions, and the only thing to do there was study. I lived in one room with my best friends, Jeno Pfeffermann and Erno Matyas. We studied together and shared one set of books. Sometimes we were invited to eat in the homes of more prosperous Jewish families. We did not eat much on other days.

Occasionally, we organized Jewish events, such as Zionist rallies, dances, and performances. We finished our baccalaureates in 1921, and went home to Sibiu for a wonderful summer with the intention of heading to the University of Vienna.

Sadly this did not apply to me. I had no money for the railroad trip to Vienna, let alone housing or living expenses. My wealthier friends had none of these problems. I hoped to join them, but I needed to earn money first. That fall, while my friends settled in at the University of Vienna, I took a full-time job with the state railroad's accounting department. All rail station cashiers sent in monthly accounts for ticket sales, and I verified the calculations and corrected the errors. It was an easy job, except that all communication was written in Romanian which I spoke but did not initially know how to write.

Those two years working for the railroad were the most educationally productive of my life. I had no responsibilities so after work I spent my time reading. Luckily, there was a German library in town with an excellent librarian to guide me. I loved Russian novels as well as Shakespeare. By reading voraciously for many years, I learned more than during all my years of formal education.

After two years at the accounting office, I moved to Cluj where I stayed with my maternal uncle Ghidaly and worked for a chalk manufacturing enterprise, doing office work and translating from German to Hungarian. Cluj had a large theater and an opera. While in Cluj, I attended *Carmen* so many times I knew the music by heart. My friends wrote me letters, encouraging me to hurry to join them in Vienna, but I was too busy reading and attending the theater, activities my peers would have considered peculiar. I was in no particular rush to leave.

Vienna: 1926–1928

In 1926 when I was twenty-four years old, I entered the University of Vienna where I shared a dorm room with my best friend, Jeno, near the *Alserstrasse.* I was often hungry and recall that Jeno would sometimes show up with some cold food or dry bread for me to eat. I had a difficult time leaving my parents. I was aware that I lacked emotional strength, but I was fortunate that I had good, devoted friends to lean on, particularly Jeno, who had an enormously positive influence on my life, more so than my parents and my other friends. Jeno was also a penniless kid from the same small town in Romania. He benefited from having an older brother, Mano, who was already a member of the university faculty.

Carousing with my best friends in my college years.

In my two years at the university, I studied in the department of philosophy (philology), and I withstood my friends' pressure to study medicine. I indulged in lectures on literature and philosophy, and continued to work hard to become a more cultured person, reading constantly and attending the theater frequently. In 1928, I became sick from influenza and had to be admitted to Rothschild Hospital. I was so impressed with the medical staff and their kindness that afterwards I followed my friends' advice and switched my studies to medicine.

At the turn of the twentieth century, the University of Vienna's

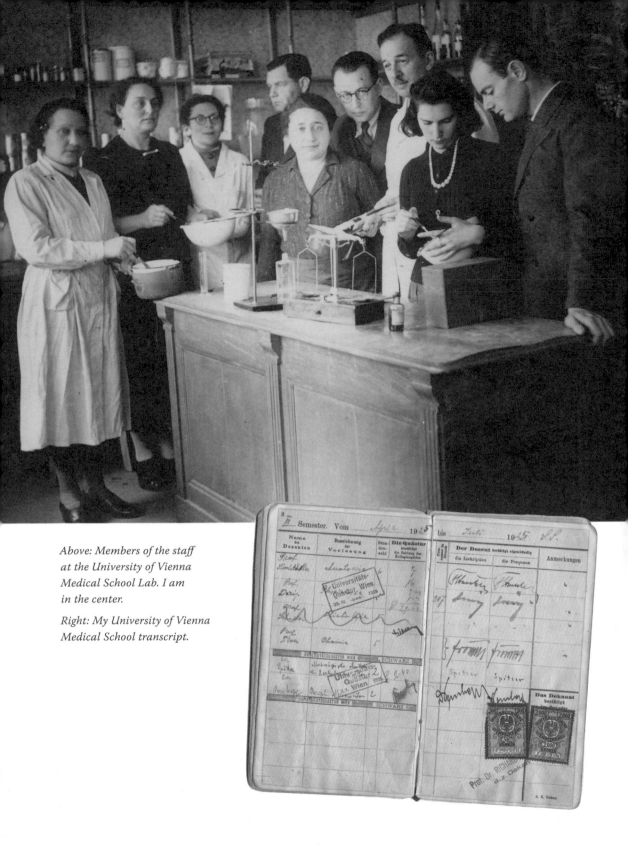

Above: Members of the staff at the University of Vienna Medical School Lab. I am in the center.

Right: My University of Vienna Medical School transcript.

medical school was one of the world's best. The faculty included several Nobel Prize winners and the founder of psychoanalysis, Sigmund Freud.

When I enrolled in 1928, Vienna's medical school was already in decline. It remained a first class medical school, attracting students and physicians from all over the world, but the most eminent scientists were no longer there. My surgery professor, Dr. Budinger, was one of the last students of Dr. Theodor Billroth, the father of modern abdominal surgery. Dr. Budinger was a remarkable man, but he did not make me a great surgeon.

My classmate, Laszlo Gonczy, introduced me to the psychoanalytical movement and to Wilhelm Stekel, a prominent analyst and an early disciple of Sigmund Freud. For two years, I received professional analysis and instruction from him. This training enabled me to practice psychotherapy for the rest of my career.

Once a week, during my five-year residency rotation, I worked in an outpatient clinic for surgical training. The professor managed the most difficult cases, and the rest were handled by me. One day a mother brought her fourteen-year-old daughter to the clinic to verify her virginity, and I asked the professor to help me with this delicate situation. Without the slightest hesitation, the professor led the girl to an examining room and had her take a seat. He looked out the window for a few minutes and never examined the patient. Afterwards, he informed her mother that she was perfectly well. The mother and daughter left happy, and I learned a valuable lesson about how to protect a vulnerable patient.

I studied in the university library or at a local coffeehouse because our dorm room was not heated. I loved Viennese coffeehouses because I could spend the entire day at a table, studying and reading newspapers after purchasing a single cup of coffee. The rest of the day, the waiter would serve me cold water, or if I could afford it, another cup of coffee or a slice of strudel.

In my first two years of medical school, I attended lectures on anatomy, worked in laboratories, and had microscopic training—all this without ever touching or examining a patient. During that time, no one cared what I did. Afterwards, I was required to take exams with the faculty in Anatomy, Physiology, Histology, Chemistry, Pharmacology, and Zoology. I got to choose the time, sequence, and interval between exams. I could take the tests in a few weeks, a few months, or not at all. No one would question me. The catch was that without successfully passing all the exams, I could not advance further in my medical training.

During the oral examination, the professor would sit in front of one or two candidates and verbally quiz them. The examiner had enormous liberty in the questions he asked and the answers he accepted, so he could quiz you in such a way as to pass you or, if it was his whim, flunk you.

"Studying" at a Viennese coffeehouse.

I once attended an oral examination of a female student by Professor Tandler who was one of Vienna's most renowned anatomists and a fabulous teacher. The examinations took place in the regular auditorium before a large audience. Students with upcoming examinations attended to learn about likely future exam topics. An assistant arrived with a tray holding an assortment of anatomical specimens including a huge penis. The professor, with a pencil in his hand, pointed to the penis. He said politely, "Please take this specimen and tell me everything you observe." The young woman reached for a glove, took the penis in her hand and said, "I have a penis here in my possession." Tandler immediately interrupted her. "Young lady, you don't possess that penis. This penis belongs to the Institute of Anatomy, please continue." The medical students in the audience broke into a roar of laughter. The professor could not restore order in the auditorium. The student lost her composure, was unable to continue, and consequently flunked the exam.

As a resident, I was solely responsible for my own medical training, which consisted mainly of examining patients and reading current medical journals. I received limited instruction from professors, assistant professors, or older residents as the faculty and staff did not pay much attention to their students. Professors made their morning rounds and were followed by a throng of students who could barely hear the conversation between the patient and the doctor. No questions were permitted and there were no discussions. The professor's conclusions were noted and the students followed with

utmost respect to the next patient. It seemed at times that the professor was oblivious to the students around him. After five years of residency, I received praise from the heads of each of the departments, but I never knew by what means they made their judgment.

Residents were responsible for anesthesia for the large number of patients scheduled for surgery each day. We used the Billroth anesthetic to induce rapid and complete general anesthesia using a combination of ether and chloroform. After securing the patient's tongue to prevent suffocation, we dripped the anesthetic on some gauze covering the patient's face. If it was too fast, the patient would die. If the drip was too slow and the patient was insufficiently sedated, we met the wrath of the surgeon. The margin of safety was extremely narrow.

During my summer vacations, I went back home to Sibiu. It was there that I had my first taste of sweet love with a young, kind girl named Margit Neu. She was from a religious Jewish family, and her father taught religion in the local public schools. Whenever I returned home, Margit was the center of my attention. Everyone expected me to marry her, especially Jeno, but unfortunately I spent so much time in Vienna that we gradually grew apart.

I had relationships with other young women as well, some of whom still lived at home. I marveled at their inventiveness, courage, and daring. To invite a man to the family apartment when a mother might suddenly return required planning, organization, and determination. My girlfriends were successful, without any surprises or interruptions.

Today, there has been a so-called "sexual revolution", but I think it is misnamed. A better description might be a sexual revelation, a removal of secrecy. Even in my day, sexual freedom was available to those who partook. If the pendulum swings back again, what we will likely observe is the return of discretion and secrecy.

Those were the days of unspoiled beautiful memories—I was loved by Margit and my parents. I had no worries, fears or insecurities. I had a rosy future and not the slightest indication of the cruel times lurking ahead. Though I had heard of incidents in which Jewish students were mistreated, it is worth noting that I personally experienced no anti-Semitism during this time.

Gisy:
1928–1934

Before the Nazi era, I was a typical university student living in Vienna. My life was carefree and unburdened. I attended lectures by noted professors, and spent countless hours with friends in the coffeehouses, studying and discussing politics, art, and current events.

My lack of money never gave me much concern. I was fully accepted and appreciated by my friends and participated in all their activities. There was no drinking in our Jewish crowd. I could not afford cigarettes, but whenever my friends lit up, they automatically handed me one as well.

I used to walk from the Eppinger Clinic to the *Allgemeines Krankenhaus* to listen to lectures. On my route, I saw an attractive girl working in a cosmetics shop. Since my arrival in Vienna, I had dated several friendly young women, but I knew immediately that this girl was special, and it took me a while to work up the nerve to converse with her.

Her name was Gisela "Gisy" (pronounced Gee-Zee) Tiger, a beautiful, charming, twenty-year-old young lady with a melodious Viennese accent—pure German, the language of Goethe and Schiller, only the melody was different, charming, and captivating. Gisy could quote pages and pages of these classic German writers by heart.

I was not a shopper, so I needed an excuse to talk with her. In December 1928, I received an invitation to a friend's house for a New Year's party, and I finally worked up the confidence to invite Gisy to be my date. After some hesitation, Gisy accepted my invitation, and we spent a memorable evening together on New Year's Eve.

This date started a five-year romantic courtship. Whenever we went out socially, Gisy had a chaperone, which was usually her oldest sister, Sophie, or her mother. We were very happy, very much in love, and we wished to get married. As was customary at that time, Gisy's parents and siblings participated in her marriage decision.

Gisy's mother was opposed to the marriage. She felt that a businessman, like her oldest daughter Sophie's new husband, Bill, would make a more suitable husband for her daughter. Gisy's father was a tolerant bystander with no influence in the decision-making. Sophie, the most reasonable person in the family, took no part in this momentous conflict. Her sister, Clara, was against the marriage, ostensibly to protect the family's reputation. Clara's jealousy was the real reason for her opposition, and she caused much commotion but did not damage our relationship. Gisy's oldest brother, Max, gave so many reasons to oppose the marriage that his advice was not considered. Gisy was my

Our wedding photo.

only ally. Because of her tremendous will, she overcame her family's opposition and got her way.

Gisy and I were married after my medical school graduation. We rented our first apartment in the *Dresdnerstrasse*, a neighborhood with both residential and commercial properties. I used the apartment as our residence as well as for my private medical office.

The apartment's entry hall was used as a patient reception area. On their way to my examination room, my patients had to walk through the kitchen that was hidden by curtains. My office hours were from 2:00 p.m. to 4:00 p.m., which was typical for the time. I made house calls. It was unheard of to call a doctor and get a recorded message, or be advised to take two aspirin and call again the next day.

My examination room had all the necessary equipment, including a desk with a good filing system and a gynecological table with an ultraviolet lamp. There was also a small laboratory that had a microscope to examine a blood smear or urine specimen and a sterilization facility for needles and syringes. After working for five years in the hospital, where nurses were responsible for equipment sterilization and syringe assembly, it was a challenge for me to do all this by myself. After work I was exhausted and I fully deserved to relax at the coffeehouse. I drank coffee and snacked on a sweet roll, reading and listening to music until Gisy returned from her job working at her mother's cosmetics shop. On occasion, we participated in the Viennese nightlife. We attended the theater and symphony and also enjoyed the many excellent neighborhood restaurants. At that time, the coffeehouses were still full of people and the theaters, opera house, and cabarets were packed.

As for my parents, I last saw them together on a visit to Sibiu in the mid-1930s. My mother had first visited Vienna shortly after I was married in 1932. She spent a few weeks with us, and was very happy to know that her son was a doctor, a common wish among Jewish mothers. When she left, it was arranged for my father to visit me the next year, but unfortunately he passed away beforehand. It is painful to me that I saw my parents so infrequently during my time in Austria.

I remember seeing my father for the last time on a cold, windy, rainy day, as I was leaving for Vienna. He did not feel well, but I didn't have the slightest inclination that this would be the last time I would see him. After his death, my mother moved to join her sister Rebi in the nearby city of Brasso, where she lived until her death. My parents were lucky to have died of natural causes at seventy before the Holocaust reached Romania.

In 1937, our first child was born, an event which gave us great joy as well as the necessary fortitude to cope with the dangers ahead.

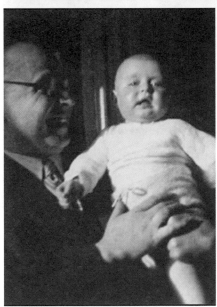

Germans entering Vienna, March 13, 1938. (All photos in this chapter courtesy US Holocaust Museum.)

The Rise of Nazism: 1934–1937

By the early 1930s, anti-Semitism was becoming more common and increasingly vicious. I believed Hitler meant every word he wrote in *Mein Kampf*. Although many Jews were in denial, I had no doubt that Hitler's threat was real and that we would have to emigrate from Austria sooner rather than later. All the Jews in Austria could hear the terrible rumblings from Nazi Germany; the horrific anti-Semitic slurs broadcasted from various Nazi rallies and in Hitler's speeches. But it was so far away. Very few politicians took the Nazi threat seriously. Churchill was the exception.

Jewish businesses were required to have signs.

In 1934, Austrian Nazis entered the Chancellery building and murdered the leader of Austria, Chancellor Dollfuss. He bled to death after the Nazis prevented paramedics from saving him. After Kurt Schuschnigg succeeded Dollfuss as Austria's Chancellor, many Austrian Jews were worried that the new government would implement anti-Semitic policies like those in Germany. Schuschnigg proclaimed that there would be no persecution of any political or religious group as long as he governed, and the Austrian Jewish community's fears subsided and many returned to their normal daily affairs.

Adolf Hitler addressing enthusiastic Viennese crowds at Heldenplatz on March 15, 1938.

During the early years of my marriage, it may have appeared that we led a comfortable middle class existence. However, the truth was that we were deeply anxious about the increasing anti-Semitism. In 1937, our first child, Susie, was born. She was lovely, cooperative, and a great joy to us. I remember looking in her crib, finding her eyes locked with mine, filled with recognition and love. Susie's early years were a happy time for us, and her presence gave us the necessary fortitude to cope with the dangers ahead.

In March 1938, Gisy and I were sitting in our elegant living room looking out the window when, to our shock and horror, we saw hundreds of German warplanes in the sky. The German annexation of Austria known as the *Anschluss* was completed in a few hours. Austria ceased to exist as a separate country; it was now part of Germany. The next day, there was a parade of Nazi troops in the streets of Vienna. My fellow Austrians wholeheartedly approved of the Nazi takeover. Many cried tears of joy.

Hitler arrived the following day for a victory celebration, and the good Austrians were so enthusiastic in shouting "*Heil* Hitler," that on the day following the celebration you would have thought there was an epidemic of laryngitis.[1] Suddenly the swastika appeared on

The humiliation of the Jews.

Viennese Nazi police prevent Jews from entering the University of Vienna.

everyone's lapel; you could hardly find anyone on the streets without it.[2]

The persecution of Jews was immediate but disorganized. Leading Jews were treated as enemies of the state and were rounded up and jailed. Other Jews were publicly humiliated. Jewish stores and homes were looted without police interference. Fortunately, Jewish women and children were not molested at that time.[3]

Jews were forbidden to practice their professions. Many found it difficult to get decent jobs. The University of Vienna Medical School dismissed me along with most of its Jewish faculty and professional staff.[4]

People in our neighborhood had customarily greeted me by lifting their hats and remarking, "*Guten Tag, Herr Doktor.*" This was accompanied with a slight bend of the head or trunk. But, after the Nazi takeover, this behavior changed. Many Austrians were now persuaded by Strasser's and Goebbels' propaganda that pure Aryans were always superior to the Jew, irrespective of their wealth or education. An Aryan prostitute was nobler than the most sophisticated Jewish woman. Racial superiority appealed to the Austrians. Our building's janitor had always been respectful but he now disdained me. He defiantly looked me in the eye and did not lift his hat as before. He exuded a new sense of pride; after all, he was superior. For my own safety, I chose to be diplomatic and feigned not to notice his altered behavior.

Some of our non-Jewish friends were embarrassed and uncomfortable, pretending not to see us; others shunned us. I vividly remember riding on the streetcar with Gisy when I saw an old friend of mine. She was a very pretty, professional dancer who was well educated and the daughter of a respected attorney. When she saw me in that streetcar, she smiled at me with unmistakable joy, but I thought it was not wise to engage in conversation with her because she was wearing the obligatory swastika on her lapel. When she got off the train at the next station, I followed her with my eyes and saw tears running down her face. She probably recognized my changed situation and felt sorry for me.

A young, attractive peasant girl cooked, washed, and cleaned for us. Her name was Mizzy Fogel and she had the saint-like appearance of a Madonna. One day Gisy found her teaching Susie the Nazi salute. The poor girl was shocked when she learned that we were Jews and were forbidden to use the salute. Unfortunately, I had to dismiss her because Jews were forbidden to employ Aryans. The peasant girl thought we were lying to her because, she said, we did not look like Jews as depicted in the *Der Stürmer* newspaper, as we lacked a hook nose, long beard, greedy eyes, or some deformity.[5]

Gisy's older sister Clara was married to an Aryan. After the *Anschluss*, Clara's husband concluded it was too difficult to be married to a Jewish woman, so he quickly obtained a divorce. Clara was traumatized. Divorce was not an uncommon result for a mixed marriage at that time.[6]

---

1   On Monday March 13, 1938, there is "a torchlit procession through [Vienna] led by the [Nazis] and there is the din of 'Deutschland, Deutschland über Alles' sung in the bars. It takes Hitler six hours to make the journey from Linz to Vienna. It takes this long because of the crowds....The Cardinal of Vienna [orders] the bells of Austria to ring." On March 15, 1938, 200,000 people jam into the *Heldenplatz*. "They cling to the statues, to the branches of trees, to railings. There are figures on the parapets silhouetted against the sky. At eleven o'clock Hitler comes onto the balcony. He can hardly be heard. As he comes to his peroration, the noise prevents him speaking for minutes on end. You can hear it all the way to the *Schottengasse*. Then: 'In this hour I can report to the German people the greatest accomplishment of my life, as *Führer* and Chancellor of the German nation and the Reich, I can announce before history the entry of my homeland into the German Reich.' 'The scenes of infatuation at Hitler's arrival defy description,' writes the *Neue Basler Zeitung*." Edmund de Waal in *The Hare with Amber Eyes (Illustrated Edition): A Hidden Inheritance* (Farrar, Straus and Giroux, 2012), 244.

"The ovation was endless. As German cameras panned across the crowd they picked out faces in sheer ecstasy, women who seemed almost orgasmic, men at the edge of bearable emotion." Thomas Weyr, *The Setting of the Pearl: Vienna Under Hitler* (Oxford University Press, 2005), 37.

2   The ballot read "'do you acknowledge Adolf Hitler as our Führer and the reunion of Austria with the German Reich which was effected on 13th March 1938?' On the pale-pink ballot there is a huge circle for *Ja* and a diminutive one for *Nein*.... In this proper plebiscite, Jews are ineligible to vote." De Waal, *The Hare with Amber Eyes*, 245.

Adolf Hitler said "'In my eyes [Vienna] is a pearl. I will give it a setting that is worthy of this pearl and place it in the care of the whole German Reich and the German people....Tomorrow, this city, and that in my conviction, will [vote] *Ja*....I believe it was God's will to send a boy from here into the Reich to raise him to be the leader of the nation so as to enable him to bring back his homeland into the Reich. Otherwise one would have to doubt God's Providence.'" 99.7% of Austrians voted in favor of a referendum for Austria's annexation by Germany. Hitler said "'This is the proudest hour of my life.'" Weyr, *The Setting of the Pearl*, 72-5.

3   According to the Austrian historian Gerhard Botz the attacks against the Jews "'consisted mostly of symbolic acts and historic rituals aimed at the destruction of a sense of identity – humiliations, abuse and arrests – but there were also physical attacks, beatings, murders and also robberies on a mass scale. It was if medieval pogroms had reappeared in modern times.' In no city of the Reich were pogroms so 'spontaneous,' so general and brutal as in Vienna." Rolf Steininger, *Austria, Germany, and the Cold War: From the Anschluss to the State Treaty, 1938-1950*, (Berghahn Books, 2012), 15.

4   On April 25, 1938, "a quota system [had] been introduced. Only 2 percent of the university students and faculty [would] be allowed to be Jewish: from now on, Jewish students [could] only enter with a permit; 153 of the Medical School's faculty of 197" were dismissed. De Waal, *The Hare with Amber Eyes*, 258. 18 members of the Institute for Mathematics and Theoretical Physics at the University of Vienna were fired as well as 50 out of 53 members of the Vienna Psychoanalytic Society including Sigmund Freud. Weyr, *The Setting of the Pearl*, 83.

5   In each copy of the *Der Stürmer* newspaper at the bottom of the title page, the motto was *"Die Juden sind unser Unglück!"* ("The Jews are our misfortune!"). In the nameplate was the motto *"Deutsches Wochenblatt zum Kämpfe um die Wahrheit"* ("German Weekly Newspaper in the Fight for Truth").

6   On May 20, 1938, the Nuremberg Laws, which were already in existence for three years in Germany, were now applied in Austria. Jews were "not allowed to marry a Gentile, have sex with a Gentile or display the flag of the Reich. [Jews were also] not allowed to have a Gentile servant under the age of 45." De Waal, *The Hare with Amber Eyes*, 262.

Preparations for Escape: 1938

Hitler cast a shadow over Europe. I recognized the immediacy and the seriousness of the danger. Having a child gave us the courage and the willingness to emigrate. I was focused on the mechanics of leaving Austria, learning a new language, and figuring out how to find future employment. Some friends and I organized a group to learn Spanish and English. I took some courses in cosmetic procedures, thinking that with my medical knowledge and some instruction in cosmetics, I could earn a living without a medical license.

Still, the majority of my Jewish friends denied the imminent Nazi threat. At this critical time, many were working to get new positions in Austria to improve their material status. Surprisingly, my colleagues' behavior continued even after several well-known professors and their assistants were thrown out of the University of Vienna without warning. Families of mixed marriages, veterans who fought in the First World War, and well-connected Jewish families who had lived in Austria for generations had a naive hope that their special status would give them protection. Jews who did not prepare to emigrate seemed to me to be blind, deaf, and dumb. My sole focus was to escape from the Nazis.

Those with foresight prepared their escape, transferred funds, and obtained the necessary documents to leave the country. Many of them, however, did not follow through quickly enough, missed the narrow window, and were caught. I had friends who were unwilling to sell their businesses for a pittance and waited for a better deal which never came.

Jews had a very difficult time emigrating from Austria-Germany. First, it was necessary to acquire an entry visa to another country before obtaining an exit visa from Germany. In addition, transit visas were also necessary to travel through other countries.

Gisy's younger brother Frank and I successfully purchased fictitious entry visas to Cuba from the Cuban Embassy. These entry visas enabled us to obtain the German exit visa but would not allow us to step foot in Cuba.

Gisy's oldest brother Max was a lawyer who had been a leader in the Social Democratic political party in Austria. In 1934, Max and a number of other Social Democratic activists were arrested, and Max was sentenced to six months in jail, where he shared a cell with a number of Austrian Nazis. As a result, he understood the nature of the Nazi threat and was successful in making his own arrangements to immigrate to England.

Enormous crowds of Jews besieged the various foreign consulates for visas, stamps and signatures. Over time, the lines outside the embassies grew in size and became

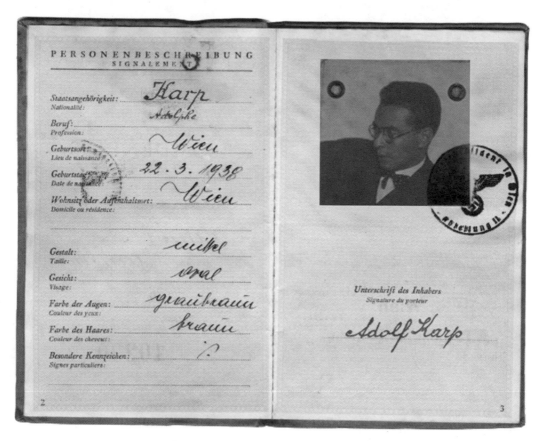

My German exit visa.

alarmingly chaotic. Jews experienced a sense of panic that they would be unable to obtain the necessary visas to leave Germany.[7]

This was the first stage of Hitler's final solution. When other countries were unwilling to accept Jews, thousands were trapped in Austria. The Jews who did not emigrate were later sent to concentration camps. This was a critical time to escape. Those who were delayed or were unsuccessful in their emigration plans died.

I knew several university professors who recognized the evil nature of the Nazi regime, but lacked the willingness or the fortitude to leave the country. They chose suicide instead.[8]

After the Nazi takeover of Austria, I knew that the Nazis' first priority was to neutralize their opposition. They arrested Jews, political opponents, intellectuals, writers, journalists, doctors, lawyers, and other prominent citizens—anyone the Nazis suspected could be an enemy. I needed to leave Germany as soon as possible, but in the meantime, I needed to hide.

Gisy had a Catholic childhood friend, Johanna Kohel, whose husband Joseph was a high-ranking Nazi official. Joseph was often absent from his home for weeks at a time due to his official business. Because Aryans were not permitted to associate with Jews, Johanna met with us secretly. She generously let me hide in her home for a few days while Gisy gathered my remaining travel documents.

In those early days, Jewish women were not harassed by the Nazis. Gisy successfully made all my travel arrangements. To emigrate from Austria-Germany, you had to prove that you owed no taxes and were not involved in any active criminal proceeding.[9] Even with a small child, Gisy acquired the necessary documents with amazing efficiency.

In my final days in Vienna, when I had to make necessary arrangements, I was very lucky that I was not detained when I was walking down the street. If I were to accidentally bump into a passerby, instead of exchanging a "pardon me" for a smile, such an incident would likely be met with a poisonous expression that was meant to kill. Had a Viennese Nazi supporter alerted an SS man nearby to me, I could have been arrested for not wearing a swastika and then sent away to a concentration camp.

These days were terrifying and our minds and thoughts were consumed by the dangers we faced. This forced us to tap into our unconscious and instinctive survival mode that has been preserved over the millions of years in our genes. We were now unbelievably alert, inventive, and prepared to defend ourselves.

---

7   "Four days after the Anschluss of Austria, in March 1938, the German Gestapo Captain Adolf Eichmann arrived in Vienna and unleashed a terror campaign designed to force the Jews of Austria to emigrate. Three thousand Jews a day besieged the American embassy in Vienna, and comparable numbers tried to obtain visas for Latin America or Switzerland. Determined not to raise the United States' slender quotas, President Roosevelt called an international conference on refugees at the French resort town of Évian-les-Bains in July [1938]....In the end, none of the nations made a substantial change in its immigration quotas and the Jews were left with expressions of sympathy and not much else." Michael Marrus and Robert Paxton, Vichy France and the Jews: with a new Foreword [1995] by Stanley Hoffmann (Stanford University Press, 1995), 58.

8   The suicide rates of German and Austrian Jews rose dramatically during the 1930s and early 1940s. The estimated suicide rates (as high as 1% per year or more) are without equal at any time in the past in any nation of the world." David Lester, Suicide and the Holocaust (Nova Science Publishers, 2005), 92-3.

9   The most important tax was called the Reich Flight Tax. Bank accounts, liquid assets and other property were taxed at 90% when Jews left Germany and were thus effectively confiscated by the German government.

Fleeing the Gestapo: 1938

June 13, 1938, three months after the *Anschluss* was the day of my departure. My travel papers were ready, including my passport and visas. All I needed was the luck not to be arrested on the way to the airport. Everything went smoothly. The taxi arrived and I kissed Susie good-bye, not knowing when or even if I would see her again. Gisy accompanied me to the airport. All my belongings fit into a small suitcase. Gisy's brother Frank and I were booked on the same flight to Switzerland, and Gisy's brother Max was at the airport for his flight to England.

At passport control, an SS man inspected my papers. He found my notes of names, addresses, and phone numbers of individuals and organizations in Paris whom I thought could possibly provide me assistance. The SS man looked at me quizzically, and then turned around to find someone else to help him examine my incriminating documents. At the same time, someone from another section called the SS man for assistance. He stamped my passport, placed my papers on the counter, and left in a hurry. I did not hesitate. I picked up my papers and proceeded directly to the plane. I found a window seat and sat down quietly, expecting the SS man to return and take me away at any moment. I saw many yellow-uniformed storm troopers on the airfield, but no one came for me, and after a short while, the plane took off, and I felt immense pleasure. It was an enormous relief that my terrible nightmare was over.

When Gisy returned to our Viennese apartment, several Gestapo (German Secret Police) officers were waiting for her at the door. They asked if I was home and demanded to speak with me. Since she knew that my plane had already departed for Zurich, Gisy responded to their questioning with uncontrollable laughter. Unsure what to make of her gaiety, the men left after searching the house and did not return.

After a few days' stopover in Zurich, Gisy's brother Frank and I arrived in Paris. It was unbelievable to walk the streets, ride the subway, and be free to move around without fear. We could eat at restaurants, walk anywhere, chat with people in the street, and interact with strangers without swastikas. I now appreciated what freedom really meant.

Fortunately we already had a safe place to live. Gisy's youngest brother Emil and his wife Greta had been residing in Paris since 1936, and kindly invited us to stay with them in their two-room apartment.

Shortly after Emil and Greta got married, they left for France, planning to travel to Spain to join the democratic forces in their struggle against the Spanish Fascist dictator, Francisco Franco. But it was too late to help the Spanish democratic opposition, so

Emil and Greta Tiger.

they settled in France.

Gisy was unprepared to emigrate. She wanted Susie to receive her necessary vaccinations. In addition, she wanted to ship our furniture, personal items, and my medical equipment to Paris. This plan turned out to be a mistake. We anticipated that Gisy and Susie would follow me with ease, but their departure was difficult and almost ended tragically.

It took three months before Gisy could leave Vienna. She got her passport, but she had trouble getting an entry visa to another country and thus could not obtain a German exit visa.

Gisy's brother Frank traveled to Switzerland. He used his connections to obtain a Luxembourg entry visa for Gisy. With her passport and visa to Luxembourg, her German exit visa was finally granted. With Susie safely in her arms, Gisy took a train to Trier, Germany, which is the border town closest to Luxembourg. The nearly empty train was under the supervision of an SS man who, miraculously, was quite friendly.

When Gisy reached Luxembourg, a border official informed her that her visa was invalid. Just twenty-four hours earlier, the Luxembourg government had revoked all prior visas, so Gisy and Susie returned to Trier. Gisy contacted me in Paris, whereupon Frank immediately returned to Switzerland and acquired a new Luxembourg visa for her. After Gisy had safely entered Luxembourg, she still lacked the necessary French entry visa.

Gisy observed that the Luxembourg locals crossed the French border every day to go shopping. This activity was done in full view of the French authorities.

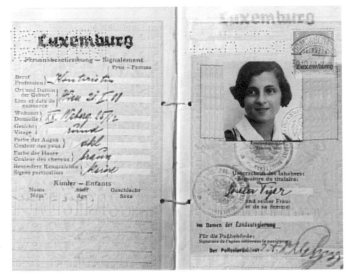

Gisy's Luxembourg Visa.

This behavior was customary for the local people but not for a Viennese Jewish refugee. After three days of plotting, Gisy bought some ordinary local clothing so she could blend in, found the routine crossing place, put Susie in her buggy, and in the most natural way, strolled across the border into France. She immediately headed to the local train station, and took the first train to Paris.

Gisy sent us a telegram to let us know she would be arriving that evening, but the message was not delivered. When the taxi dropped her off at our apartment building, Frank, Emil, Greta, and I were at the movies. When Gisy rang the bell no one answered. It was late, she was in a strange neighborhood with a baby and she did not know what to do.

Typically, when someone rang the bell late at night, the concierge would pull a lever next to his bed that unlocked the front door. Gisy did not know about this arrangement and kept ringing the bell. The concierge realized something was wrong and came to the door where he met Gisy with the baby. He made them both comfortable in his apartment, and when we returned from the movies, I was overjoyed to find my family waiting for me.

Emil and Greta's little apartment could not accommodate all of us. Gisy and

I rented a small wooden three-room house in Chelles, a suburb of Paris, on Rue Sergent Triaire. The house came with Pompon, a cat that later became Susie's pet. Even after we moved with Pompon to a more "luxurious" place, the cat regularly returned to the old wooden house.

Susie and Pompon.

Paris: 1938–1940

After arriving in Paris, I registered with the Prefecture of Police and applied for a permit to stay in the country. I was concerned to discover that each permit lasted only seven days. Luckily, this renewal process was routine, and after each permit expired, I returned to the police station for a new one. This practice went on for years.

Gisy and I tried to acclimate to our new world because there was no going back.

Gisy taking vocational classes at ORT.

Each day, I took the bus to Paris to the old hospital, Hôtel Dieu, where I attended hospital rounds and lectures and did my best to stay current with medicine.

Gisy spoke French but I did not. To learn the language, I read newspapers, went to the movies, and struck up conversations with strangers. Learning French was not easy for me. Not only do the French, and Parisians in particular, dislike foreigners in general, but they especially dislike hearing foreigners misuse their language with a foreign accent. This intolerance surprised me because France in the 1930s had been very generous in accepting political refugees from around the world.

The Hebrew Immigration Society provided food, medical care, and monetary support to Austrian Jewish refugees. I met the organizers and they offered me a job in their medical office.

We had no money, so I needed to work. I not only saw the refugee patients at the medical office but I also provided care for a small number of wealthy French patients. I was trained in Vienna to be a psychoanalyst, but I did not want to be limited to this field exclusively. Gisy persuaded me to combine medicine with psychoanalysis, and I have done so ever since.

An ophthalmologist on one occasion performed a cataract operation on my kitchen table. It was successful, but I feared there could be trouble if we continued to perform such procedures in my home, so we never did it again.

Another Jewish organization, the Office of Rehabilitation (ORT) offered vocational training. Gisy took classes in leather work, while I continued to study cosmetics. That winter, we settled into our little wooden house and kept in touch with Gisy's family. Gisy's oldest brother, Max, secured a position at Hull College teaching Roman law. Max was incredibly resourceful and he successfully arranged in short order for Gisy's parents and his sisters, Clara and Sophie, to immigrate to England.

At the time, we were busy trying to survive our everyday circumstances. In Chelles, our house was unheated; only the kitchen had a stove. Early one morning, we realized the water in the sink had frozen and ran in a panic to check on Susie. We found her sound asleep, well wrapped in warm blankets.

Not far from our home in Chelles was a settlement of White Russian refugees who had lived there since the Russian Revolution in 1917. I tried occasionally to speak with them in my rudimentary French but they did not speak French at all, and they still lived with their clothes and most other belongings packed in suitcases. After more than twenty years of exile, they remained ready to return to Russia at a moment's notice.

Despite lacking both a proper doctor's office and a French medical license, I established a thriving medical and psychoanalytic practice. I met my patients by making house calls, and surprisingly no one complained about my peculiar way of practicing medicine.

The local pharmacist filled my prescriptions, which were written on plain notepaper. I assumed the authorities were unaware of my activities, until one day the bell rang, and a police officer entered holding my medical case. "Doctor," he said, "you forgot your bag in the pharmacy, and Mrs. Durant thought you would need it."

The French Foreign Legion: 1939

In 1939, I volunteered to serve as a doctor for the French infantry in the event that war with Germany broke out. I volunteered because, ironically, I thought it would be safer for me in the French army in wartime. Foreign civilians, in particular those of German and Austrian origin, were already treated with suspicion and I feared arrest. Spies were everywhere and the police could not distinguish Jewish refugees from secret agents.

Sure enough, immediately after World War II began in September 1939, French authorities confined foreign refugees to internment camps. Unlike my peers, I reported for duty with the French infantry. The officer in charge inspected my papers carefully. He observed that I was an Austrian citizen and said, "My dear doctor, you are not a Frenchman, and therefore, your voluntary enlistment is invalid. Only Frenchmen can serve in the French army."

I said nothing and waited to be dismissed. The officer watched me in complete silence and likely sensed my fear and dread of being interned. He then reached into his desk drawer, pulled out a small booklet and said, "If you desire to serve France, I can help you fill out an application for the French Foreign Legion. If you pass a physical exam in Lyon, you will be sent to one of the Legion's camps in Africa for training and service. If you enlist, your service will last only for the duration of the war instead of the normal five-year term. Those that finish their service with the Legion can become French citizens."

I could not refuse the officer's generous offer to join the Legion, as the alternative was a French internment camp in Melun. So after discussing my options with Gisy, I returned the following day and enlisted with the Legion. All the Legion recruits were sent by train to the Lyon processing center, which was housed in Fort Vancia, an old structure built in the 1870s that was surrounded by crumbling walls.

We assembled and waited in a muddy, unpaved courtyard. A sergeant arrived and commanded us to follow him to a large barracks where he ordered us to stand in line for a customary army inspection. It soon became obvious that the sergeant was drunk, but he still behaved like a five-star general. He stopped in front of each recruit and inspected us very carefully in our civilian clothing. Then he told three of us to step out of line and stand in a corner. He gave us no explanation, only a short remark to the effect that we didn't belong with that scum. Then he commanded all of us, including our elite group, to return to the muddy courtyard. He distributed filthy tin bowls and spoons, accompanied by much shouting. When all of us had utensils in hand, the sergeant ordered complete silence. "Drop all bowls and spoons to the floor!" No one followed the order. He repeated it and all utensils were immediately dropped to the floor. He looked around, satisfied with our introduction to military discipline. With a smile he said, "Pick up your plates and get your food in the kitchen."

There was no water in sight to clean the utensils, so I skipped the meal and took a walk. In a short while, everyone was told over the loudspeakers to proceed to the kitchen and peel potatoes. I did not follow the order and instead continued my stroll. No one stopped me; there was no supervision of any kind.

I wandered into the Legion's medical office and met an older German Legionnaire. He had served in Marrakesh for many years, with the scars on his forehead and cheeks to prove it. He told me he had a large stab wound in his side as well. We had a pleasant

My French Foreign Legion document.

talk, and he informed me that, because of the surge in recruits, there were no sleeping quarters for new arrivals. When I told him that I was a doctor, he offered to let me sleep in the barracks with the medical team. Only floor space was available, but it was clean, and he gave me an extra blanket.

At my physical examination, the medical officer measured my height and weight but did not draw blood or request a urine sample. I informed the officer that I was a physician. After a few seconds of contemplation, he told me that I was physically ineligible for military service as there were other younger and fitter candidates, but I could work in the medical office with him and examine new arrivals. He was working alone and my assistance would make his life easier.

I accepted the job and was given a desk and a stethoscope but no uniform. My new career did not last long. A few weeks later an inspecting, higher-ranking officer asked why a civilian doctor was examining Legion candidates. He demanded to see my papers which had a notation that I was "not fit for military service in the Foreign Legion," so he immediately discharged me from my duties, and the next day I was sent back to Chelles.

On my way home, I stopped in Paris and made my way to a public bath. Since arriving in Lyon, I had not properly bathed. There had only been a cold faucet for washing. The public bath in Paris was a delight. After cleaning up, I rushed home.

When I returned to Chelles, I was the sole remaining male refugee in town. All of the other male foreigners had already been sent to detention camps. The police soon became aware of my presence and, very shortly, I too was sent to a nearby internment camp in Melun.

My Life in Detention Camps: 1939–1940

The Melun detention camp was surprisingly well organized. There was a daily roll call, regular meals, and minimal surveillance. The captain who ran the camp warned us that we would be shot if we cooperated with the enemy. Clearly he was uninformed about his prisoners, most of whom were Jewish refugees who despised the Germans.

However, there were a few non-Jewish German sympathizers in the camp. They would count the number of French planes flying to the battlefield. I was angry when they gloated that only half the French planes returned intact.

Late one night, the sentry on duty for our barrack at the Melun camp entered our sleeping quarters making much commotion and swearing at the top of his lungs. He waved his loaded rifle about wildly and promised to shoot all German SOBs. Just like his superior who oversaw the camp, the sentry was oblivious to the anti-Nazi views of his inmates.

The fighting came closer to us each day. After a few weeks at the Melun camp, we inmates were evacuated and packed onto three separate trucks, each going in different directions. Miraculously, my one small suitcase was put on my truck. After a short ride, we boarded a train to an unknown destination. We traveled south then headed west, close to the Spanish border.

Early the next morning, while the train was idling at a small station, a soldier entered my compartment and ordered me to follow him off the train. Immediately afterwards, the train started moving, leaving the two of us alone on the platform. The soldier refused to answer my questions about why I had been removed from the group or what was happening to me. We walked in silence for a few hours before arriving at a building with a crumbling, six-foot-high wall and a large wooden door. After knocking several times, we were escorted into an office where an officer sat behind a dilapidated desk. The soldier handed this officer an envelope with some papers, saluted, and then exited.

The officer inspected each paper in my file. He appeared particularly interested in my military book and a picture of my wife, Gisy. He then opened a file cabinet, removed a large box, and took out a number of photographs, always comparing them with the passport photo of my wife. After he compared all the pictures in the box with Gisy's photo, he replaced the box and took out another, and inspected all those photographs as well. Then he opened my small suitcase and carefully inspected its contents. He tapped the sidewall and bottom of the case, and after not finding anything suspicious, he closed it. He handed the suitcase back to me and asked me to follow him. On leaving the office, I noticed a sign on the outside of the door—*Sûreté Militaire* (military intelligence).

The officer returned my suitcase but kept my documents. He informed me that I was now an inmate of a special camp for former Foreign Legionnaires who were citizens of Germany or other Axis countries. I was told that I would be imprisoned here indefinitely, and allowed no visitors or correspondence with the outside world. These restrictions did not trouble me. I figured Gisy had already left Chelles, and must be on her way to southern France ahead of the advancing German army. Because our mutual whereabouts were unknown, I could not communicate with her anyway.

I was sent to the barrack where I was provided with a bed, a thin blanket, a small pillow, a shelf, and a chair. In comparison with Lyon, my lodgings did not look too bad! Relieved, I sat down on my bed and looked around. It was early morning, and all the beds around me were occupied. I was exhausted, so I took off my shoes, got into bed and immediately fell asleep.

It must have been noon before someone shook me out of my slumber, handed me a traditional metal food container and spoon and said, "Eat. Your food will get cold. It tastes bad the way it is, but when it is cold, even the dogs won't eat it."

It had been quite a while since I had eaten anything, so I ate with relish. The man who had given me my ration watched me so closely that I felt uneasy. I tried unsuccessfully to make conversation. Finally he asked me, "Did you see what you have on your shelf?" I looked and saw a bottle of red wine and a pack of *Gauloises Bleu* cigarettes. "They are yours," he said. "They are your daily ration, as you know."

As a matter of fact, I did not know. Now I understood my neighbor's interest, but he was a diplomat of sorts, and our talk diverted to other areas. He said to me quite frankly, "What are you doing in this Legionnaire camp? You are not a Legionnaire."

I explained to him how, just a few weeks ago, I had worked for the Legion in Lyon. After hearing my story, he became less suspicious, and our conversation took on an easier tone. He said that while I was sleeping, he and his buddies had looked me over and concluded that I was a spy put in the barrack by the Legionnaire administration. I did not look like an ex-Legionnaire and seemed out of place. After many years of service in Africa, typical ex-Legionnaires were covered with scars and permanent skin discoloration on their faces and bodies from sun exposure.

When I told him that I was a doctor, he relaxed and introduced himself as Karl. He got down to business and asked me if I drank wine or smoked. "No," I said, although I used to smoke occasionally.

"So, doctor, I have a proposition for you. If you give me your daily ration of wine and cigarettes, then I will help you. I guarantee no one will touch your stuff except for your soap ration. Soap is stolen here with such efficiency that my own ration is never safe. But don't worry, I have all the soap we need." (I suspected he was one of the soap thieves.) "I will also wash your laundry and bring you your chow. Trust me. You will get better portions when I take care of it."

My new "partner" was a strong, muscular man with a reckless expression, but his eyes revealed a glimmer of decency, despite some very rough years. I accepted his offer and gave him my wine and cigarettes. We remained very good friends, and his services were very helpful later on, even when no compensation of wine or cigarettes was available.

Order to report to internment camp in Melun.

My life in the camp was tolerable for the brief period I was there. I had no responsibilities and spent my time reading and improving my French. The ex-Legionnaire camp was small, totaling less than one hundred prisoners.

The inmates were all old Legionnaires with visible signs of their former employment. Some had legs amputated and replaced with wooden stumps that served them well enough to walk. Others had black eye-patches or faces distorted by wounds with poor surgical repairs. These men were not an aesthetically pleasing sight, but I got used to it. Surprisingly, these ex-Legionnaires who had fought for France for years in various wars showed no sign of resentment about being placed in a French internment camp.

Every day, the detained young men would get into violent and bloody altercations over trivial matters. The other Legionnaires would stand in a circle encouraging one or the other to fight. Bloody noses and open lacerations were common, as was gushing blood. These fights were only punishable when the bleeding was so bad that the combatants needed serious medical attention. The injured were then transferred to town for suturing, and the culprits ended up in the docks, with all their special privileges of wine and cigarettes temporarily withdrawn.

The authorities let these fights go on, perhaps realizing that they were a good way of letting off steam. If no serious injuries occurred, the contestants shook hands and the spectators clapped. It was not unusual for the officers and guards to applaud as well.

Much to my surprise, there was another Hungarian Legionnaire in my barrack. We became so friendly that one day he revealed his "secret"—that he had in his possession a piece of dried-out paprika, which he kept wrapped with the utmost care in a piece of questionably clean cloth, and tucked into a secret pocket like a precious stone. He told me the paprika was so strong that when it touched your tongue, it burned like hell. He generously offered it to me, but I could not deprive him of this special pleasure.

There were many detention centers for refugees in Europe. The numerous other French camps were not desirable places—some smaller, some very crowded, most of them unsanitary with very poor food and water supply. The detainees in those other camps were treated with indifference. By comparison, this Legionnaire camp was a resort. We had no assignments, no duties or chores, and for me with my private "butler," it was like a vacation.

Outside the camp, there was a beautiful small lake with clean water that we used for bathing. The camp officers seemed oblivious to it, and the "elite" Legionnaires would sneak out for a swim when there was a warm and sunny day. Karl was among the elites and I joined because I was his protégé. No swimming trunks were available, but nobody cared.

In early June 1940, with the German army rapidly advancing, it was clear that our stay in the camp would be short. Our daily luxury of reading the smuggled-in newspapers suddenly ended. There was no more lax management; the staff observed roll calls and paid closer attention to the rules.

We heard rumors that the Germans were advancing down the Atlantic coast to the Spanish border, and soon afterwards the camp was evacuated. We were put on trucks and taken to the same train station where I had arrived only a few weeks earlier.

This evacuation was surprisingly well organized. We each had our luggage placed in the proper train compartment with several days' rations of bread, canned ham, canned fish, and fruit jelly. There was no wine but there was the usual ration of cigarettes.

Nobody knew where we were going. All I could tell was that the train was heading southeast near the Atlantic coast. During the day, I could glimpse the names of some train stations: Oloron, Bayonne, back to Oloron, then off to Pau, Tarbes, Lourdes, Tarascon, Arles, and Montpellier.

Spending the night on the train was difficult. We could see the German flares in the distance, but we did not know the meaning of their different colors. It was clear enough that the Germans were very close. To our surprise, the train kept moving.

One night we saw the German army in the very near vicinity. I knew the end was near. It would be just a matter of minutes before the train was stopped and I would be a German prisoner. My fate was sealed. I opened my small handbag and told the fellow sitting next to me that I would no longer need my belongings. Not questioning my motivation, he gladly accepted my gift that included warm socks, handkerchiefs, a clean shirt, and some other items. I regretted this generosity days later, when I badly needed these irreplaceable luxuries. The train headed in a northeasterly direction. Finally, we arrived in Nîmes.

We disembarked and began a long march. My friend Karl was of great help and carried my suitcase. After crossing the hilly countryside, we arrived in the middle of a large, empty field. There was flat grassland as far as the eye could see, with a few bushes here and there. The only sign of human habitations was a small farmhouse in the distance. To our great relief, we saw no Germans.

We sat on the grass and waited. More people arrived in trucks and on foot and soon the field was full of people. They were all refugees, living in France, who had been evacuated from their camps. To my surprise, I found friends from Melun and Chelles. It was like a homecoming.

We were a big crowd of people assembled on an empty field with nothing else in sight, not even barbed wire, and no military personnel—nobody except refugees with their belongings. A few hours later, French military personnel arrived with wooden poles, green cloth, barbed wire, and thick string. Karl told me that this material was used to build marabouts.

"What are marabouts?" I asked. Karl explained they were circular tents, generally used in Africa in desert expedition warfare. He told me that they were very strong and provided excellent protection against wind and rain. Within a few hours, the Legionnaires had assembled large circular tents that each provided shelter for twenty to thirty individuals. They distributed blankets, and to my amazement, the camp was ready to house hundreds of people. Even food was arriving. Each tent had a large tin bowl in the middle. We received our usual metal containers and spoons, and that was it. We went to sleep.

The camp had no water or sanitary facilities so we all snuck out to the camp's periphery, and with no spectators in sight, took care of business, hoping that by the next day more suitable latrines would be available. It was not to be. The lack of sanitary facilities was a serious problem, and many detainees became quite sick. There was no medical help available and no medications whatsoever. For those who sought my advice, I could provide verbal assistance only.

Escape was still possible. Although I did not know where to go, it probably made sense to leave. Some people simply left their belongings and walked away. No one stopped them; no one was brought back. The camp was very unpleasant, and at some point there would likely be a visit from the Gestapo. Nevertheless, I leaned towards staying because the camp staff had my military book, passport, and other travel documents. I also thought it might be easier to get in touch with Gisy because I was known in this camp, and Gisy might be able to find me here.

I contemplated my escape for three days. On the fourth day, barbed wire was installed, and there were now armed guards. I could no longer escape easily. I slept much better and could think clearly as I now had no choice but to stay.

The fighting war between France and Germany had been very brief. The German blitzkrieg invasion began on May 10, 1940, and within just 3 weeks, the French army was pushed to the English Channel. Their British allies were forced to evacuate the continent at Dunkirk. The French gave up Paris without a fight and declared it an open city. The Germans entered Paris on June 14th without resistance. Three days later, French Marshal Pétain announced, with a "heavy heart," that the war was lost and that fighting would cease. The armistice was signed on June 22, 1940, allowing Germans to occupy two-thirds of France. Southern France would be administered by Pétain in Vichy.

The French army was to be disbanded, and the French military personnel were not permitted to carry guns. Soldiers all over France carried only batons instead.

Our camp outside of Nîmes was located in Vichy France, and was thus not occupied by the Germans. The camp functioned quite well, even after the French surrendered. When the fences were built, the guards and sentries came. The French administration set up their offices in the adjacent St. Nicholas farmhouse. Every morning, barrels of water in large wine casks were brought to the camp in a cart pulled by two horses. With very limited supplies, you had to decide how to use your daily water ration. One day you washed, the next you did laundry, and you always saved a small amount to drink.

Disease flourished at the camp and there was an immediate outbreak of intestinal disease that spread rapidly. To my astonishment, the camp commander seemed indifferent to the problem, even though an epidemic could affect the surrounding areas and nearby cities. My repeated complaints to the authorities were met with anger. The commander waved his baton furiously, clearly unable and unwilling to do anything.[10] [11] At the center of the camp, the inmates set up a "market," where people offered their old possessions such as a knife, watch, book, old shirt, purse, or belt. The sellers would then exchange their goods for cash or more desirable "junk."

Karl remained loyal to me even though I had no rations of wine and cigarettes to pay him. His quarters were in a different section of the camp, but he often visited my tent and brought me newspaper clippings or gossip. Karl was resourceful and

I often saw him with cigarettes and alcohol.

One day, he came in a hurry, bringing me news of the arrival of the Gestapo. The Germans reviewed the list of detainees and left with some of the refugees. These men were never heard from again. Luckily, the Germans had not yet organized the systematic roundup of Jews in France, they were looking for specific individuals.[12]

My top priority was to find my family. It was a constant and burning worry that I knew nothing of the whereabouts of my wife and child. They were surely uprooted and in flight from deadly danger. I knew that all foreigners had been evacuated from Paris and that they must be moving south, away from the war zone like so many millions of others. Fears dominated my days and nights. Would I ever see my family again?

The problem was that Gisy and I had not previously arranged an address to write to each other. While other people had relatives in different parts of the country—an aunt, a grandmother, or an old friend—and thus could make contact through letters, we had no way to contact each other. But I was not alone. Whenever refugees passed train stations, city halls, or public buildings, they left notes on walls for lost relatives and friends, with addresses to make contact.

During my stay in Chelles, I provided medical advice to the Leitner family before Mr. Leitner was sent to a detention camp. His wife remained in Chelles, and he maintained contact with her through one of his relatives. Later, Mr. Leitner was transferred to my camp in Nîmes and when he got sick, I provided him medical care. In one of his letters to his wife, Mr. Leitner mentioned that I was his doctor once again.

---

10 Mortality at the French-run internment camps varied between 5-10%, which was catastrophic by modern Western standards, but not comparable to a death camp like Auschwitz that had a 97% mortality rate. Marrus and Paxton, *Vichy France and the Jews*, 176.

Also see the article "The Nutritional Situation in the Camps of the Unoccupied Zone of France in 1941 and 1942 and its Consequences," in the New England Journal of Medicine, March 15, 1944 written by my colleagues at the Marseille medical clinic René Zimmer, Joseph Weill and Maurice Dubois. In the article, the authors found that internees at the French camps averaged only 950-1100 calories per day or 40-50% less than the local French civilian population. The malnutrition caused morbidity that resembled a virulent epidemic of a communicable disease with increasing morbidity in the first stage, reaching a plateau in the second stage and then finally falling off in the third stage. The low caloric intake was further compounded by a lack of protein in the diet. A typical meal of stale vegetables served in soup form with an attendant lack of vitamins resulted initially in sickness and eventually death.

11 Lion Feuchtwanger, a German-Jewish novelist, was interned with me at the same camp in Nîmes. He wrote, "That is why I do not attribute our misfortune [in the St. Nicholas camp in Nîmes] to any deliberate intent. I do not think that the Devil with whom we had to deal in the France of 1940 was a particularly truculent devil who enjoyed practical jokes of a sadistic nature. I am inclined to think that he was the Devil of Untidiness, of Unthoughtfulness, of Sloth in good-will, of Convention, of Routine, the very Devil to whom the French have given the motto '*je-m'en-foutisme*'—'I-don't-give-a-damn.'" Lion Feuchtwanger, *The Devil in France: My Encounter with Him in the Summer of 1940*, Feuchtwanger Press, 2008, 53.

12 There were some very well-known anti-Nazis in our camp who were very distraught over the Surrender on Demand clause (Article 19) in the Armistice agreement between France and Germany. It said that the French Government is obliged to surrender on demand all Germans named by the German Government who are living in France.

Gisy's Escape: 1940

Gisy had her own extraordinary journey in wartime France.

On June 12, 1940, the Prefecture in Chelles ordered all foreigners to leave town within twelve hours. Gisy suspected this order was made because the German army was rapidly advancing towards the town. Black smoke could be seen all the way from Chelles to Paris as the French had ignited gas and oil tanks to slow down the German advance. Gas masks were distributed to the adults but not to the children, and were required to be carried at all times. Since Gisy only wished to live as long as Susie was alive, she emptied her canister at the first opportunity and filled it with small food items for Susie.

Gisy's sister-in-law, Greta, had begged Gisy to pick her up at her apartment in Paris. When Gisy was delayed, Greta, in a panic, hurried to the train station without her, and when Gisy arrived at the apartment, Greta had already departed. Gisy was furious that Greta had abandoned her, particularly because she had gone so far out of her way to pick her up. Gisy and Susie headed to the train station, hoping to travel south away from the German army. There were thousands of people at the station and no trains were available. It was nearly impossible to maneuver Susie's baby carriage because of the desperate crowd. But Gisy was tenacious, and she stood on the train platform for two full nights until the next train arrived.

The chaos at the train station was unimaginable, as there were hordes of frantic people trying to get out of Paris. Because of her extraordinary persistence, Gisy got on the next train. She did not know the train's destination, but she observed that it took her southwest toward Bayonne.

Gisy decided to sail to Africa to get as far away from the war as possible. She knew there were ships headed to French North Africa leaving from St. Jean de Luz, which is located just south of Biarritz, on the Bay of Biscay, on the southwest coast of France. But when she arrived in this picturesque small town, she discovered that the port was packed with refugees with similar travel plans. The ship's captain made an announcement that there would be no food or water available during the African voyage, so everyone left the dock and went to the town center to shop for necessities.

Gisy saw oranges in a store window. Recognizing that the store had already closed for the day, she banged on the door. When the store owner saw Susie in her buggy, she opened the door and gave Gisy some oranges and lemons for their voyage.

When Gisy returned to the little harbor, the ship was already completely full and was ready for departure. Angry and exhausted, she returned to town to wait for the next boat to Africa, which was expected the following day.

Gisy and Susie spent the night sleeping on the floor of a vacant store. Early the next morning, she was back at the dock waiting for the arrival of the promised ship, but no boat arrived.

The following night, Gisy found that her vacant store was now taken by others so she made her new "residence" in a coal storage shack. Coal and coal dust covered the entire floor, but at least there was a roof. She spent the night there with Susie sleeping in her buggy.

The next morning there was an article in the newspaper that the ship Gisy had missed two days earlier had been bombed by German warplanes. Others said that the ship had been destroyed after it hit a mine. In the fog of war, no one was quite sure of anything except that there were no survivors. Over the next few days, the armistice terms between France and Germany were negotiated, and as a result, no more boats would be allowed to depart for Africa. Disappointed but not discouraged, she needed a new plan.

Gisy proceeded to the town of Oloron. Here refugees from northern France slept in schools and public buildings. These places had been specially prepared to meet the immediate needs of the mass of civilians fleeing from the advancing German army.

Gisy pushed Susie's pram across the Bordeaux region. She started in Biarritz and stopped in Oloron, where she found shelter for a few days in a kind French woman's attic. She then continued until she reached the town of Pau. As in Oloron, the Pau town hall housed refugees overnight on makeshift bedding made of straw. One morning, subsequent to eating a warm breakfast that was provided by the town's elderly, the foreign refugees were separated. They were forced to board buses to an abandoned and dilapidated, walled-in castle located outside of town. When the refugees stepped off the bus, they were required to hand their travel and identification documents to a waiting official.

The refugees sought out a place to rest but the castle had only bare rooms lacking beds, blankets, or any basic comfort. During the day, people congregated in the castle's courtyard, which was surrounded by a crumbling wall. Gisy noticed a barely visible, ivy-covered door.

The castle inmates organized themselves without official interference or direction. An aggressive bully took control. He distributed food and water, assigned sleeping quarters and so on. Gisy concluded that the situation was untenable and planned her escape. That first night, while everyone was asleep, she took Susie and left through the courtyard's ivy-covered door. Gisy fled unobserved, pushing the buggy ahead of her.

On the rural road back to Oloron, a local farmer and his wife offered Gisy a ride in

Document from the city of Oloron permitting Gisy and Susie to stay in town for two weeks.

their wagon. These modest farmers took in Gisy and Susie for a few days and shared their meals with them. The farmer's wife urged Gisy to properly register with the local Prefecture of Police. Because she had given most of her documents to the officials at the castle, Gisy's only remaining document was a fragment from a copy of a police order that required her to leave Chelles. It had an official appearance with a signature and stamp that surprisingly satisfied the Oloron town clerk, who tore off a scrap of paper and wrote a single sentence. Giselle Karp and her child had permission to stay in Oloron for two weeks. He signed it, placed the stamp over it, and wrote down the dates. Gisy could now stay in Oloron legally. She was enormously relieved because, after weeks of continuous movement, she could now begin her search for me without fear of arrest.

In wartime France, communication was nearly impossible for refugees. People seeking loved ones left notices at train stations and on the walls of public buildings. Every wall quickly became covered with such inquiries. Gisy placed her own note in several locations, requesting information about her husband, Dr. Karp. She went to the local train station daily to see if anyone had left a note. She was quite despondent until, one day, she received a simple reply from Mrs. Leitner. "Your husband is in a camp with my husband somewhere near Nîmes."

With this new information, Gisy made immediate plans to travel to Nîmes. Unfortunately, rail travel was now strictly forbidden for civilians because the few trains available were reserved solely for military personnel. But she did not despair and, without hesitation, Gisy approached the Oloron train station supervisor for help in traveling to Nîmes. She told him that she was aware of the civilian train restrictions, but she hoped that he would assist her. Gisy showed the supervisor Mrs. Leitner's note about my presence in Nîmes. After noticing Susie in her pram, he said, "Wait here until I have a chance to help you." Gisy settled in the reception room, made Susie comfortable, and waited and waited. Hours after dusk, she told the supervisor that it was difficult for her to stay indefinitely with a 2-year old child, and she promised to return the next day.

Gisy spent that night with Basque farmers who were in Oloron temporarily. Her new friends were overjoyed when Gisy told them that she had found the whereabouts of her husband.

Gisy was persistent and appeared daily at the station. Several days passed but no train stopped. Finally, the supervisor informed her that a train would stop later in the day. In a great hurry, Gisy took emotional leave from her Basque friends, returned to the station, and waited.

There was no train schedule. The station attendants had only general information, which changed quite often. However, this time the announced train arrived, stopped, and a large number of tall, black soldiers disembarked. They were African Senegalese men. The station supervisor placed Susie's buggy on the train, and in a short while, they were on their way. All the compartments were third class, but Gisy made Susie comfortable. Gisy was in a very hopeful and jovial mood as she was finally on her way.

She faced her traveling companion who was a giant black Senegalese soldier. He gave Susie a pleasant smile and conversation ensued. The soldiers offered Gisy some kind of canned fish and a piece of baguette. Gisy was hungry and helped herself and then promptly fell asleep.

Susie was wearing a light pink jacket and matching cap, all meticulously washed. As the train rumbled through the countryside, Gisy noticed after she woke up from her nap that Susie's jacket collar and cap had changed color from pink to black. She first assumed that the change in color was due to dust, but then the dust began to move. Susie and Gisy were both covered with fleas. Gisy swatted them away, but the fleas were relentless.

Toward evening, Nîmes came into sight, and it was a great relief to get off the train. Like every town in the south of France, Nîmes was packed with refugees. Gisy searched for a hotel room, but the only rooms available were rented by the hour and were not used for sleeping.

Fortunately, it was a clear summer evening so Gisy chose to spend the night in the open. Gisy found a coffeehouse with some chairs on the terrace. She packed Susie in her buggy and tried to get some sleep. That night mosquitoes mercilessly attacked both of them. Gisy was successful in keeping them away from Susie, but the bugs concentrated their fury on her. When morning came, her face and arms were covered with so many welts that she could barely recognize herself. But Susie had slept well, knowing nothing of the desperate battle.

Gisy's mission was to find my camp. She made inquiries with locals in town, but no one had heard of any camp in the area. So she sought assistance at the local military headquarters. The entrance was guarded by two sentries with wooden sticks. She persuaded them to let her enter and gain access to the senior military official in charge.

The captain asked Gisy a barrage of questions about her past, her husband's role in the war, and the reason why he was detained. It was clear that this officer was unaware of the problems affecting foreign refugees. The fact that I was in the Foreign Legion and had ended up in a detention camp was incomprehensible to him. A lieutenant was present during this interrogation, and Gisy noticed that he seemed amused. After more questioning, the captain announced there was no camp in that region, and he dismissed her.

The lieutenant smiled very pleasantly at her and asked, "What are you going to do now?" There was no maliciousness in his attitude, but Gisy sensed that this man knew more than the captain. Shortly thereafter, he admitted to her that he knew of the camp, but it was against orders to reveal its precise location.

Gisy needed the lieutenant to violate his duty. Without sufficient money for a bribe, Gisy chose to use her feminine charm. The conversation turned to lighter subjects, and at least in Gisy's telling of the story, she received the following proposal: After work, the lieutenant would take her to a nice restaurant with extraordinary wine. The lieutenant told her that after the date, he would show her the way to the camp the next day.

Gisy said that she needed to make sure he really knew the camp's location, so the discussion continued until she had all the necessary clues. He disclosed the camp's distance from Nîmes, its direction northwest, and the road which led there. Gisy surmised that most likely the lieutenant did not know any more details. She agreed to the rendezvous that evening, but after they parted, Gisy proceeded directly to find the road leading to the camp. It did not take long and she left town, pushing her buggy in the camp's direction. It was not easy maneuvering because the street was unpaved and it started to drizzle. Passing farmers gave her wagon rides for short distances, and in this way, she advanced steadily, determined to find the camp by nightfall.

The local farmers knew the camp's approximate location. She was to turn off the rural road near a specified intersection and proceed up a hill. After walking for an hour or so, she heard a dull noise in the distance, a human noise, and knew that she must be going in the right direction. As she advanced, she saw dust that covered a large area, and smelled the unmistakable odor of an open latrine. She followed these leads.

After some time, she found the barbed wire fence that surrounded the camp. Shreds of soiled newspaper and human excrement covered the fence line. She walked around the barbed wire enclosure until she found a soldier holding a wooden stick guarding an entrance.

Gisy asked the sentry at the gate if her husband was there, but he did not know me as there were hundreds of detainees. The sentry could not ask his superior until evening when the change of guards took place. Nearby detainees joined in the discussion, but none of them were aware of my presence at the camp.

It was very unusual for a woman with a small child to be at the gate. My old friend Karl heard about the female visitor and came to check it out for himself. When Karl realized who she was, he quickly persuaded the sentry to allow Gisy access to the camp. Karl then escorted Gisy directly to my tent.

Like so many detainees, I was very sick with some sort of intestinal disorder. I was lying on my blanket when Gisy and Susie entered the tent. I was so surprised and excited to see them that I immediately felt much better. Gisy was shocked by my appearance because I had lost so much weight after limiting my diet to only bread and an occasional egg.

Gisy made an immediate decision to get me released from the camp. Without delay, she went to see the camp's commander and told him of my predicament. He offered to have me transferred to a hospital, but she convinced him that all I needed was a doctor and some medication. So she demanded and obtained for me a 24-hour leave for medical attention in Nîmes.

Karl packed up my few belongings in my dilapidated suitcase. It would not close, so Karl rescued me again. He cut a thick rope that was holding up a nearby tent and used it to bind my suitcase securely. Karl joked that when the wind picked up, the tent would surely collapse. He then carried all my belongings to the gate. I had become quite fond of Karl who was a fighter and jack-of-all-trades. Although I was preoccupied with my family, I noticed that Karl had tears in his eyes and I gave him an emotional embrace before we separated and left the camp.

I felt like a free man. As we were walking away, I examined my family more closely. I saw that Gisy looked the same; she had good color, even though the mosquito bites were still clearly visible. Susie looked as lovely as ever with her beautiful, dark, suntanned complexion, but I was concerned that she had not grown since I'd last seen her. I mentioned this to Gisy, who cleared up the mystery by pointing out that it had only been eight weeks since our separation. Because of all the movement, my worries and the danger, I felt as if a very long time had passed since I had last seen my family.

We walked down the hill toward Nîmes in haste. It was already late in the afternoon, a mild pleasant day, and we were thrilled to be together again. At sunset, we arrived in Nîmes. Gisy knew from the previous day that no hotels were available, so we asked private citizens for overnight shelter. Gisy walked with Susie on one side of the street, and I walked on the other. We figured our chances were better with Gisy and Susie in her buggy without my presence, as I had not bathed for weeks.

Just before nightfall, Gisy approached a lady on the street who said that she had a room for rent and was willing to take Gisy into her home. Then Gisy pointed to me on the other side of the street and informed her that her husband was part of the bargain. The women looked me over in shock as I had been wearing the same clothes for the past few weeks, but she did not object. She took us to her very nice apartment with a bathtub, and we felt that we had arrived in paradise.

Our new landlady was Mme Roulet, a school teacher. She lived alone in her apartment because her husband was a prisoner of war in Germany. Her daughter was caught behind the divided zone in northern France and was staying there with her grandmother. It gave her great pleasure to have a child in her home, and we soon became good friends.

Marseille: 1940–1941

The chief of police in Nîmes informed Mme Roulet that due to the recent influx of foreign refugees in town he had been ordered to round them up and place them in detention camps. Mme Roulet promptly helped Gisy acquire a round-trip "pass" from Nîmes to Marseille from a well-meaning local official. Unfortunately the *Sûreté Militaire* had kept my papers at the St. Nicholas interment camp outside of Nîmes, so the official was unwilling to provide me with a round-trip pass. We were told that the police in Marseille checked incoming travelers' papers at the train station and would arrest refugees without valid documents.

Mme Roulet advised us that we could sneak into Marseille by bypassing the local police checkpoint. She suggested that we access an unguarded door located at the far left hand side of the Marseille train station that was restricted to station personnel. In view of the imminent danger of arrest, we had little choice but to board the next train to Marseille and take our chances at the station.

The train compartment was standing room only. Everyone wanted to get to Marseille. It was seen as the "promised land" because there was an American consulate, rail links to Switzerland and Spain, as well as a port with its opportunity for escape.

When we arrived at the St. Charles train station in Marseille, a mass of people queued to exit. We noticed that the civilian police were carefully inspecting each person's papers. The lines moved very slowly, so we had ample time to look for the unguarded door Mme Roulet had told us about. No one was watching us, and we walked all over searching for the "magic" door. But we could not find it.

Many passengers remained in line at the main exit, waiting for their papers to be inspected. We joined the line and advanced to the exit where two policemen guarded the door. I took the middle line between the two men. Gisy stood behind me. On the spur of the moment, I decided to use one hand to help her with the buggy. With my other hand, I reached into my inner pocket, a motion feigning that I was replacing my papers, as though they had already been inspected. This gesture with my hand fooled the policeman. He noticed the movement, assumed that the other officer had inspected my documents, looked at Susie, and waived us on. I often marvel at the success of this completely unplanned and impulsive act that allowed me not to be arrested. Incredibly, we were allowed to enter the city of Marseille![13]

As in Nîmes, hotel accommodations were unavailable in Marseille. We spent the day looking for a room and entered an elegant hotel that was already completely booked.

The clerk saw Susie in the pram and was sympathetic to our desperate situation. He asked us to wait in the lobby while he made some telephone calls. Afterward, he offered us a spare mattress in the attic storage room. We gladly accepted.

Our quarters were used as a depository for broken hotel furniture. We found a mattress on the floor, covered with a clean sheet and a blanket. A water pitcher and two clean glasses were by its side. We were happy that we had a roof over our heads, and we went immediately to sleep.

We were told that we might find an affordable place to stay in the *Vieux* (old) *Port*. The next day, we proceeded towards the harbor, walking along the main boulevard *La Canebière* with the most elegant shops, hotels, restaurants and apartment buildings.[14]

Along the waterfront were many coffeehouses, their terraces overlooking the Mediterranean, filled with patrons. It was hard to believe that only a few days before, the French army had surrendered to the Germans. It seemed to me that the French people had not yet internalized what had happened to them. In those early days, there was a wide selection of food available. Waiters served cakes, café patrons ate sandwiches, and you could smell the aroma of grilled fish from the restaurants. No one appeared to have any worries. But I knew this *"joie de vivre"* would not last for long. There would be

The Vieux Port *in Marseille.*

Bundesarchiv, Bild 1011-027-1473-05 | Foto: Vennemann, Wolfgang | January 1943

terrible consequences for the French now that the Germans were their new masters. *Vae victis*! (Latin for "woe to the conquered.")

Marseille's main street La Canebière.

We walked past the port's chic neighborhood, turned westward, and entered a different world. Here were small, winding, narrow streets, and a chaotic maze of buildings, populated by Algerians speaking French with a strange accent. These intonations, from multiple continents created by interactions among seafaring people landing in Marseille, were French with an Italian melody mixed with a touch of Algerian Arabic.

In the distance, we spotted an intriguing street that was wider than the others but still not more than eight feet wide. The clean, cobblestone-paved street was structured like a staircase. It had uneven stairs which were only wide enough for one person to pass at a time.

The houses in this neighborhood were old and run-down. People were milling around, talking, smoking, and shouting, but we were not scared. We kept walking until we found a hotel above a busy tavern. The proprietress showed us a room, which we took without hesitation. We were happy to get such a bargain, and we paid her a week's rent in advance. The room had two beds and a worn-out carpet but it was large and clean. I went back to our previous hotel's attic and picked up our belongings. The hotel clerk informed us that we were not going to be charged for sleeping in the attic. I was thrilled because we had so little money at the time.

We settled down in our new apartment, anticipating a peaceful night. But it was not to be. The building across the street was so close to us that, when you looked out the window, it appeared as if we shared the same room as our neighbors. Only the gap of the street separated us. Directly across were two women dressed in provocative attire, but it was summer so we did not think much of it. When evening came, we put Susie to sleep. As we prepared for bed, the racket started. The tavern music became louder and everyone began to sing. We felt as if we were sitting at the bar and not lying in bed.

But that was the least of it. We couldn't help but observe the goings-on across the street. Our neighbors were a mother in her late thirties and her very attractive, teenage daughter.

They both wore brightly colored, alluring dresses with low décolletage. They wore a lot of jewelry, large earrings that hung down to their shoulders and looked like wheels, and necklaces with shiny, colored stones. The combination of the clothing and jewelry gave them a sense of elegance and self-confidence, and an overall good impression.

Soon, I first saw the daughter and then later the mother in their room, always with different men. The lights went on and off with the change of partners. When the women returned to the tavern below, our neighbors greeted them with great enthusiasm, and the women's voices mixed with the singing, and the racket increased even more. One interaction was particularly impressive. The girl shouted loudly down to the tavern below, "Mama, Mama," until her mother shouted back, "What do you want?" "Come right up, Mama. The man wants you now."

When we brought Susie to France, she was just a little more than a year old, and she was two when we arrived in Marseille. French was her first language, and Susie ably picked up new words and gaily repeated expressions used by our neighbors across the street, words that were inappropriate for our everyday use. Gisy was so upset that she wanted to move out immediately. Common sense prevailed, and Susie eventually forgot those vulgar phrases.[15]

A street in the Vieux Port.

Bundesarchiv, Bild 101I-1027-1473-31 | Foto: Vennemann, Wolfgang | January 1943

After sunrise, the street quieted down and we hoped to finally get some rest. Just down our street at the port's edge were tents with large tables where fishwives hawked their fresh catch during the wee morning hours. From the bargaining, I learned the true meaning of the expression "loud like a fishwife." Shortly afterward, water flowed down the street, which was an ingenious and simple method to wash the fish market. Our street was aptly named *Rue de la Pêche* or Fish Street.

The *Vieux Port* was the headquarters for thieves, muggers, traffickers in narcotics, document forgers, and murderers. It was a very poor, closely knit community. The houses had underground connections, making it easy for criminals to hide. The French police were rarely seen in the *Vieux Port* because it was dangerous and there was little chance of catching anyone they sought.

Gisy with our landlord M. Gamel at the Mascotte Hotel.

Shortly after our arrival in Marseille, we contacted the local Jewish charitable organization and received some money to cover our immediate needs. They also gave me a job at their medical clinic. I was happy to be earning a salary and also to be working again, enjoying the respect and affection of my patients. We decided to move to *Rue Poids de la Farine*, which was closer to my clinic. Although the neighborhood was quiet at night, we heard noises from the adjacent, unoccupied room. After a few days, we figured out that the room was infested with rats. Fortunately, we now knew better than to pay rent in advance, and we left immediately for other accommodations.

We chose the small *Mascotte Hôtel* on the *Rue Molière* across from the Opera. Our room was on the top floor—furnished with a large bed, a table, four chairs, a commode, and there was even a small kitchen with a single gas-burner stove. In addition, I rented three small private apartments at the hotel in case we needed to hide from the French police.

The owners of the *Mascotte Hôtel*, M. and Mme Gamel, were both unsavory. M. Gamel was a greedy man who often tried to collect our rent twice for the same week and relented only after his wife assured him that we had already paid. After the war, I learned that M. Gamel was convicted for collaborating with the Germans.

Mme Gamel was a thief. We suspected that she stole Gisy's gold necklace while she was babysitting Susie. But Mme Gamel liked Susie and Gisy, and despite her questionable morals, she was capable of kindness. She was also well-connected. Gisy and I recognized that, in order to survive, we would need to expand our social circle beyond the Jews and doctors we knew. People are complicated. Good and bad can coexist, and we chose to cultivate what was good in Mme Gamel. Later, she was instrumental in helping us plan our escape from France.

At that time, Marseille was administered by the Vichy French government and was not occupied by the German army. However, since the armistice the French police in Marseille cooperated with the German secret police or Gestapo in their persecution of the local Jewish population. It became a regular event for foreign Jews to be rounded up in the street or arrested in their hotel rooms.

Marshal Pétain, the Chief of State of Vichy France, visited Marseille on December 3, 1940. When state security was perceived to be at risk, the police expanded their net beyond foreign Jews to include all foreign refugees. To ensure Pétain's safety, the local police raided all hotels and arrested as many foreigners as they could. As we learned later, all the arrested foreigners were transferred to large ships waiting in the harbor. Foreign Jews who were arrested and those foreigners whose papers were not in order were transferred to an internment camp.[16]

On the day of Pétain's visit, Gisy went shopping and did not return home at a normal time. It got late and Susie was hungry, so I prepared a meal and fed her on my lap. Suddenly, the door to our room opened and two policemen in civilian clothes burst in. They demanded to know where the child's mother was and why I was feeding the child. I remained completely calm and informed the police that I was alone with Susie and that there was no one else to feed her. The two policemen held a short conference and then exited, never to return. That evening, the French police arrested all of the other foreigners in the hotel, which was now completely cleared of its Jewish, Polish, Russian, and Greek tenants except for the three of us.

The police had cordoned off both sides of the main street for Pétain's motorcade. Gisy was not permitted to cross the street until after Pétain had passed. Had she been successful and arrived home before the roundup of foreigners, I most certainly would have been arrested with the other hotel occupants. Susie had saved us again. When Gisy got home, I told her about the interrogation, and only at this point did we get nervous and emotional.

Days later, we heard a loud threatening voice in the neighboring hotel room. "Let me see your papers. Where are you from? What are you doing in Marseille? Do you have any relatives? Where do you work?" When we peeked out our door, we saw that our neighbor's door was partially open, and there was no chance of sneaking out without being noticed. It was peculiar that we heard no answers to the questions, and after a while, all was quiet. We later figured out that the tenant was telling his friend about his previous encounter with the police. I was very frightened by this "theater," probably because of my own recent police interrogation in the hotel. The real danger from days before had left me cold. With great relief, we went to sleep.

A city ordinance required that garbage be placed daily in front of the hotel between

5:00 a.m. and 6:00 a.m. I usually did not follow the rules and instead put out the garbage the night before. One cold and snowy evening, I deposited a big bag of garbage on the curb, directly in front of a watching policeman who gave me a written summons to appear before a judge. With much trepidation, I arrived at court on the appointed day and hour with Gisy and Susie.

We entered an immense hall filled with people. A typical offender was accused of urinating in public. It was evident that we were going to have to spend the whole day there until my case was called. Knowing from our past experiences that the French had a love for children, Gisy pinched Susie on the arm so that she began to cry hysterically. The judge immediately called me forward and within seconds my case was dismissed.

Although I had never been a practicing Jew, this Yom Kippur was different. I felt an intense solidarity with my people, and contrary to my previous habits, I went to temple. It was a very crowded service, because many Jews felt the need for prayer. The imminent danger was clearly on everyone's mind.

Gisy knew that the French police, under the orders of the Gestapo, would round up Jews on any occasion. When I did not come home by a reasonable time, she feared that I had been arrested. She raced to the synagogue. Gisy was pregnant at the time, and probably as a result of her fear and physical exertion, she went into labor. Gisy was hospitalized and gave birth prematurely to a baby boy. Due to the nursing staff's neglect and indifference, our only son died. Our grief was intense. Gisy never fully recovered from this loss.

---

13 Madame Roulet was correct; there was a magic door except we were looking in the wrong place. Varian Fry wrote that if you arrive "to Marseille by train, you could avoid the police check-up by going into the station restaurant through a service corridor to the Hôtel Terminus. If anyone asked you what you were doing (something which never happened), you could say you were going to telephone, or to wash your hands. Once you were in the hotel you could walk out onto the street exactly like any guest." Varian Fry, *Surrender on Demand* (Amazon Digital Services, 2013), Kindle location 376 or p. 15.

14 Marseille was a very cosmopolitan city of 700,000 people. It could beat "Jules Verne's record for around the-world travel: standing on its famous thoroughfare the *Canebière*, you could see the whole world in eighty minutes, as faces and costumes from every origin passed you by." Simon Kitson, *Police and Politics in Marseille, 1936-1945* (History of Warfare (Brill)) (Brill Academic Publishers; Lam Edition), 2014, 31.

15 "Marseille had long held an international reputation for prostitution." Soldiers "awaiting transport to an overseas location or sailors whose ships docked in the port were frequent customers. Immigrant workers who frequently arrived without their wives also represented a potential clientele....It was never hard to identify a prostitute in the doorways or bars in Marseille: the red glow of a cigarette in the mouth; a particular way of laughing, half–spiteful, half-mocking; a silk vest; pink stockings; short-skirts and high-heeled shoes were the signs of the trade." Kitson, *Police and Politics in Marseille, 1936-1945*, 6 and 44.

16 "It has been estimated that 20,000 individuals were imprisoned not only in the regular jails but also in four boats, four barracks and three cinemas specially commissioned for the [Pétain visit], living off a diet of stale bread and uncooked meat whilst the Head of State sat down to a seven course lunch." Kitson, *Police and Politics in Marseille 1936-1945*, 86.

Our Desperate Attempt to Obtain Visas: 1941

Our primary objective was to immigrate to America. To do so, we desperately needed to obtain entry visas from the American Consulate in Marseille. For one reason or another, we were regularly denied. The vice consul told us that there were several new regulations issued in Washington. New immigrants were required to have a material guarantee from a sponsor to insure that immigrants would not burden the government. The sponsor was required to prove his financial ability with tax receipts and bank affidavits. In addition, immigrants had to prove that they had blood relatives in America.

The frequent introduction of new regulations had the effect of further limiting Jewish immigration. Thousands of people who could not meet the necessary requirements were caught in the Germans' web and ended up in crematoriums.[17]

Luckily for us, Gisy's brother, Frank, and her sister, Sophie, already lived in the U.S. Unfortunately, we had lost contact with them even though we had sent several letters to them and other members of the family. We desperately waited for some correspondence with our American relatives as they were our only hope for American visas.

Then one day we received a telegram from Sophie that included a reference to La Crosse. It took us a few days to comprehend that she

Gisy's eldest sister Sophie and her husband Ignaz (Bill) Falber promise to support the Karp family in America.

Gisy and me in Marseille.

was now living in Wisconsin and that La Crosse was the name of the town. Sophie agreed to help us and she worked tirelessly to provide us the necessary affidavits and sponsorships. Sophie was Gisy and Susie's blood relative, but I had no American relative, so I would have a more difficult time obtaining a U.S. entry visa.

Gisy refused to leave Europe without me. She could have done so years earlier because of her Austrian origin. The U.S. Immigration Act of 1924 had limited the annual number of immigrants admitted to the U.S. based on country of birth. The quota was limited to 2% of the number of immigrants from the relevant country living in the U.S. in 1890. My Romanian birth was problematic because the American immigration quota for Romanians was only 603 people per year.

Without our knowledge, Frank had implemented a risky plan to solve my "blood relative" problem. Frank wrote to every man with the last name of Karp in the Chicago phone book, asking them to sign an affidavit that they were related to me. When a man named Elmer Karp received Frank's written request, he notified the FBI. The FBI immediately sent a cable to the State Department's Immigration Office, and the Consulate in Marseille was informed that my visa request should be deferred until the FBI completed its investigation of me.

I was totally unaware of the FBI investigation that immediately affected my entry visa application. Mr. Bredford, the American vice-consul in Marseille, was now visibly relieved that he no longer had to request additional documentation such as sponsors or paid passage receipts. Instead, his new answer to me was always, "Sorry, no visa can be granted, period." With apparent pleasure, the bureaucrat simply said, "No!"

At the end of our first year in Marseille, we were running out of time and the danger was acute. We had to figure out quickly what the problem was with my visa application.

---

17 The Russell Act, passed by Congress in June 1941, stated that if an American consul has reason to believe an alien endangers public safety, then he is obliged to refuse a visa. This determination shall be automatically reviewed by the State Department in Washington. The Russell Act effectively shut down the visa process for the second half of 1941, and by the end of that year, only a few dozen visas were being issued per day. The United States was better than most countries. Canada almost completely excluded Jews, and the British shut down immigration to England and Palestine for fear of igniting anti-Semitism. Marrus and Paxton, *Vichy France and the Jews*, 114.

MARSEILLE

1940

Life in Marseille: 1941–1942

The winter of 1941 was unusually cold, and we had difficulty keeping our apartment warm. The cause was a mistral, which was a violent northerly wind that swept down on Marseille from the Rhone valley adding discomfort and headaches for many. This cold wind penetrated our clothing and we avoided doing chores outside. In our apartment, the only heat came from a small stove in our tiny kitchen, so we wore overcoats and covered up in blankets to keep warm.

Food was scarce. The Germans demanded that French agricultural products be sent to Germany and to the war front. It was a time of real hunger in France. Food was rationed, and we had to use food stamps in restaurants and grocery stores. Bread was severely restricted and in short supply. There were different rations for school children, and Susie got tickets to buy milk and eggs. Unfortunately, the tickets were not particularly useful because shops did not have sufficient supplies. Frequently, Gisy stood in line for hours and left empty-handed.

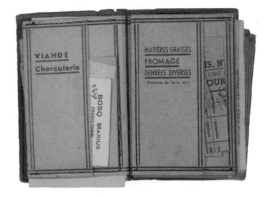

Unused food ration coupons from Marseille.

One of my patients was a Greek man with a small restaurant near our hotel. Occasionally, we would eat lunch there without needing to provide him the necessary ration tickets, and he would sneak a nice slice of meat under a heap of vegetables. My medical advice was the only compensation for his generosity.

Gisy made friends at a store where ravioli was prepared daily. When an extra supply was available, they would give her some without taking her ration tickets. We discovered a small department store that sold Coca-Cola which did not require ration tickets. We bought Susie Coca-Cola every day, grateful for the sugar it provided. The caffeine did not bother her.

On milder days, we took Susie for long walks outside the city limits. We visited farmhouses and knocked on doors, offering to buy food. We were not the only ones, and often we were unsuccessful, but when good fortune smiled on us, we returned in the evening with ham, eggs, cheese, or a big piece of bread. It was a real feast. Our hotel room was often frequented by friends and acquaintances, and sometimes, after these trips, we could offer them bread or cheese to share with us.

I worked each day at a medical clinic managed by a combination of relief agencies that included the Unitarian Service, the Quakers, and the Jewish Children's Aid Society, which was primarily funded by the Jewish charity the American Joint Distribution Committee.[18] The clinic offered general medical consultations as well as specialized medical care. There were radiology laboratories, dental care facilities and social work offices. The clinic even had a medical library and frequent lectures attended by sixty local Jewish doctors who were now forbidden to practice because of the anti-Semitic acts of the Vichy government.[19] René Zimmer managed the health center on behalf of the Unitarians. He was an Alsatian anti-Nazi who was incredibly committed to helping the Jewish refugee community.

I was very happy to be employed and earning a salary, but also of great importance to me was the respect and affection I received from my patients. Because I had a job with the clinic, I received the necessary papers so I could walk around with less fear of arbitrary arrest. It was customary for plainclothes police to ask people walking down the street for identification and permits. Tourists are generally unmolested, but individuals who look out of the ordinary are harassed. Luckily I was never questioned by the police and did not have to use my documents. Several months after leaving the internment camp in Nîmes, a fellow inmate brought me my military papers and I now had official documents which would be critical to my visa application.

Over time, I secured some psychotherapy patients from well-to-do families in Marseille. One was the French Jewish multi-millionaire Monsieur Guggenheim who lived in the *Hôtel Canebière*, which was the finest hotel in town. Mr. G was a man of extraordinary talent, a big risk-taker who had made and lost his fortune several times. During the war, he managed a very profitable wholesale tobacco business that succeeded as a result of his excellent connections with Algerian tobacco exporters. During one of his medical appointments, Mr. G took a phone call and negotiated an incredibly complicated tobacco transaction involving tens of thousands of dollars. Without taking any notes, he ar-ranged tobacco deliveries at various locations with different prices, often speaking in code. When he got off the phone, I asked him how he could remember so many details, and he offhandedly remarked that this is how he routinely conducted his business.

He once told me that the price of cigarettes would skyrocket the following week and that I should buy all the cigarettes I could purchase. So I acquired as many cigarettes as possible with my limited savings, stacking them against one of the walls in our room. Sure enough, the price of cigarettes surged and I made a sizable profit.

I found out later that Mr. G sold tobacco to both sides during the war. One day he disappeared, and I heard conflicting rumors that he was either executed by the French underground or by the Gestapo. Mr. G was the kind of man who could make a fortune in times of peace or war, but in his case, it ended badly.

Life in Marseille became more dangerous. The French police received orders from the Gestapo that a certain number of foreign Jews had to be turned over daily for deportation. They rounded up people on the streets or those standing in line for food. Those with identity papers, such as I had, were safe for awhile.

Anti-Semitic laws called the *statuts des Juifs* were passed by the Vichy government as early as October 1940. These racial laws severely undermined the rights of French Jews and allowed for foreign Jews to be interned.[20]

The Vichy government defined a Jew as someone who had two or more Jewish grandparents.[21] To obtain an exemption, you had to show tangible proof that you were baptized prior to June 25, 1940. [22]

Living in the unoccupied zone of Marseille was still much better for Jews as compared to residing in German-occupied Paris. As of April 26, 1941, Jews in occupied France were prohibited from working in a job that had contact with the public. Jews were forbidden to work in retail sales, restaurants, hotels, transportation, and banks. Similar work restrictions were later implemented in Vichy France. A few months later, Jews were banned in all of France from being public servants or working in theater, radio, film, or the press, and there were limitations on practicing medicine and law.

Jewish property rights in real estate and commercial enterprises were severely limited and most Jewish businesses had to be liquidated, causing disastrous economic consequences for their Jewish owners.[23] In addition, art owned by Jews was pillaged. Jews were also banned from possessing radios and bicycles, which were seized by the French police. Jews were even prohibited from walking on the main Parisian boulevards such as the *Avenue des Champs-Élysées*.

Most Jews were prohibited from teaching in French schools or universities. In June 1941, the French Minister of Education set a quota of 3% for Jewish enrollment in each individual professional school or university to prevent unreasonable Jewish representation in any one occupation.

On the night of October 2, 1941, seven Parisian synagogues were burned to the ground. On May 29, 1942, all Jews in the Occupied Zone over the age of six were required to wear yellow stars labeled Jew. In Vichy France, Jews did not have to wear yellow stars, but beginning in December 1942, they were required to have the word Jew stamped in large red letters on their identity cards, which would prove to be catastrophic later.

Beginning in July 1942, Jews were prohibited from visiting restaurants, theaters, cinemas, libraries, museums, historical monuments, sporting arenas, public swimming

pools, or public parks. Jews could not use public telephones and could only shop in stores in the late afternoon after scarce or rationed items would likely have already sold out.[24]

With these anti-Semitic regulations, we feared the increasing pressure of German influence in the unoccupied zone where we now lived.

We did not feel safe in the city of Marseille and we thought that we would face less risk of being picked up by the police in a suburb just outside of town. So we moved out of the *Hôtel Mascotte* and rented a small house in the northern town of Mont Olivet. The proprietress, Mme Batholme, was a short, stocky woman who lived alone. She occupied one room at the street level, which had previously been used as a garage. We rented the unfurnished main house and bought second-hand beds, a table, and a few chairs.

The mosquitoes were a big problem because our windows lacked screens. The mosquitoes favored our ceiling because I suspect they felt safe there. But these little critters did not appreciate my blood lust for revenge due to their incessant attacks on my family, and in particular Susie. I got hold of a broom and banged that ceiling, exterminating every last one of them and then went to sleep with great satisfaction, unmolested throughout the night. In the morning, we saw that the ceiling was splattered with blood. Mme Batholme came later in the day to see what had caused the disturbance the previous night. She became furious when she saw the ceiling's condition, and she demanded that we move out immediately. It was not an easy task to dissuade her.

My daughter started her pre-kindergarten class in a school close by, with a lovely teacher who gave her much attention. She learned to read and write at a young age.

On July 31, 1942, we planned Susie's fifth birthday party. We invited our friends from Marseille. Most of them would not attend; the few who did were scared and restless. Our friends were aware of raids on Jewish community centers, synagogues, schools, and other places where Jews congregated. After a short while, our friends left. They were frightened to death and went to hide.

The streets and hotels were constantly searched. The wholesale chase of Jews in

Marseille and its near vicinity was now in full swing.[25]

At this point, we decided to move again because we thought the landlady would probably turn us over to the local police. I hated this woman, and she was the only person we had met in France who was even mean to Susie. So, after paying Mme Batholme the next month's rent in advance as she demanded, we snuck out while she was sleeping. We put our most important belongings in Susie's baby carriage and left everything else behind. Mme Batholme was unaware of our destination because, had she known, she would have surely informed the authorities. I was so certain of her malicious character that in the days before our departure, we slept with our clothes on so that we could escape quickly if necessary.

We moved to one of the first floor rooms of Monsieur Ventre's old picturesque farmhouse. Our new landlord was a retired policeman and a patient of mine. Next to the outhouse was a wooden shed where Monsieur Ventre collected all kinds of odds and ends in the most orderly fashion: nails, string, lamp and clock parts, as well as buttons and pins.

The basement of the farmhouse was rented to a very quiet Italian family who had lived there for many years. To my amazement everyone in the family spoke only Italian and no French.

In the back yard, there was a small chapel with an altar, holy pictures, a cross, and candleholders. Mme Ventre prayed each day in the chapel and was a devout Catholic. She was very kind to us and willingly shared her kitchen with Gisy.

The elderly policeman pretended not to know, in the tradition of his former occupation, that we were illegal Jewish refugees. The Ventres took great personal risk because it was against the law to harbor foreigners, especially Jews, without properly notifying the local police. They readily accepted us, although we worried that their mentally disabled, 18-year-old daughter would give away our presence—not maliciously but from ignorance.

The farm consisted of a dozen fig trees whose fruit was sold when ripe in the markets of Marseille. Susie loved eating the fresh figs which were a great delicacy. The orchard had a wall that gave protection from stray dogs and not much else, as well as a fence with several rows of wire. With Mme Ventre's help, we cut a small opening in the fence behind some bushes, and we thought, with a great deal of naiveté and optimism, that in case of a police search, we could hide in the adjacent forest until the search was over, but it never came to that.

I would travel by street car only occasionally from Mont Olivet to the medical clinic in Marseille, because it was getting too dangerous to walk around Marseille. The Jewish Agency was informed of my whereabouts so my identification papers were kept up to date. I tried to stay busy and used my time reading French books to improve my language skills, often lying in the grass next to the fence in a picturesque farmhouse setting.

18 The Unitarian Service Committee ("USC") also assisted many Jewish refugees with their U.S. visas and other documents to emigrate from France. In 1941 the Reverend Charles Joy who ran the USC asked the Austrian-Jewish artist Hans Deutsch to design a chalice with a flame to symbolize the organization's values of helpfulness and sacrifice. "When Deutsch designed the flaming chalice, he had never seen a Unitarian or Universalist church or heard a sermon. What he had seen was faith in action—people who were willing to risk all for others in a time of urgent need. Today the flaming chalice is the official symbol of the Unitarian Universalist Service Committee and the Unitarian Universalist Association." See the chalice stamp on the letter on page 75. See http://www.uua.org/beliefs/chalice/flaming-chalice

19 Samuel, *Rescuing the Children: A Holocaust Memoir*, Kindle Location 1877.

20 "The Jewish population of France, less than [90,000 in 1900], had more than doubled by 1930 and stood around 300,000 in 1939. Yet even at its highest, the proportion of Jews in a French population of 41 million strong remained unimpressive: about 0.7%. Most of the French never saw a Jew or wouldn't know one if they saw him, but few, if challenged in 1930, would lack a view of Jews. Churchgoing Catholics knew them as the people who killed the Son of God—a faux pas of which Easter Week provided annual reminders. The urban populace, especially in Paris, connected them with capitalism and capitalist exploitation or else with low-paid competition that cut even closer to the bone. But there was too...'an anti-Semitism of principle-latent and quite general'....The Jews were not as other French; they were not French whatever passport they might carry; they were simply 'other.'" Eugen Weber, *The Hollow Years: France in the 1930s* (W.W. Norton, First Edition, 1994), 102-103.

"Anti-Semitism was not a new phenomenon in France" but discrimination was "at odds with the tradition of equality and religious freedom that grew out of the 18th century Enlightenment and the Revolution of 1789 and that legally prevailed in the 19th and early 20th centuries." Charles Paul in Vivette Samuel's *Rescuing the Children: A Holocaust Memoir* (University of Wisconsin Press, 2013), Kindle location 283 or p. xxiv.

Vichy broke "the legal links that normally offered protection to citizens and visitors.... Even though he never pronounced the word 'Jew' in a public statement, Marshal Pétain lent his immense prestige implicitly to a systematic propaganda of collective degeneration. Two years of governmental measures that linked national revival to anti-Semitism dulled the consciences of many French people toward a group officially blamed for everything from high prices to the defeat [by the Germans]." Marrus and Paxton, *Vichy France and the Jews*, 369.

Pétain in 1940 said that the loss to Hitler was due to internal French rot and decadence by "'anti-France' forces: Communists, Jews, foreigners, [and] Freemasons. There was no point in trying to save the country by fighting the occupier, since the defeat was a symptom and not a cause. The first priority was to regenerate French society from the inside by excluding the 'impure' elements considered to be responsible, and by bringing together the pure elements around such traditional values as work, family, fatherland, order, and piety." Denis Peschanski, "*Vichy Singular and Plural*," Sarah Fishman (editor) and Laura Lee Downs (editor), *France at War: Vichy and the Historians* (Bloomsbury Academic, First Edition, 2000), 110.

21 Technically [a Jew] under the Vichy code had to have three or more Jewish grandparents or anyone who had two or more Jewish grandparents who was married to a Jew. Attending synagogue or practicing Judaism was irrelevant to whether an individual was considered to be a Jew under the French law; thus, the code was based on "race" and not religious views. See Richard Vinen, *The Unfree French: Life under the Occupation* (Yale University Press, 2007), 142

22 In communication between the Vatican and Pétain, the Vatican ambassador said that "the church would not start any quarrel over restricting certain citizens' access to jobs or over limiting Jews' actions in society. The church's quarrel with fascist and Nazi 'racism' rested on their refusal to agree that a Jew ceased to be a Jew upon conversion to Catholicism and on their refusal of intermarriage even after conversion." Robert O. Paxton, *Vichy France: Old Guard and New Order, 1940-1944* (Columbia University Press, 2001), Kindle location 3191, 3197 or p. 175.

23 In the Vichy legislation, the "stated purpose was to 'eliminate all Jewish influence in the national economy.'" The individuals who acquired businesses at a discount as well as its competitors profited from the liquidation of the Jewish businesses. Paxton, *Vichy France*, Kindle Location 3252 or p. 179.

24 Marrus and Paxton, *Vichy France and the Jews*, 238.

25 On June 30, 1942, Adolf Eichmann, the German Gestapo officer in charge of liquidating Jews, went to Paris with a directive from Himmler that all the Jews in France were to be deported to concentration camps in the East. The Final Solution for France had begun. On July 16, there was a roundup of more than 6,000 Jews in Paris who were temporarily detained at the Vel' d'Hiv indoor sports arena. One hundred Parisian Jews committed suicide in lieu of capture. The Vichy French leader Pierre Laval informed US diplomat Tyler Thompson in August 1942 that "these foreign Jews had always been a problem in France and the French government was glad that a change in German attitude towards them gave France an opportunity to get rid of them." Marrus and Paxton, *Vichy France and the Jews*, 220, 228, 250, and 251.

The queue at the American consulate in Marseille in late 1941. (Courtesy of US Holocaust Museum)

Getting a Visa

G isy and I visited the American Consulate every day with the vain hope of getting my entry visa; however, my requests were continually rejected. Everyone at the Consulate knew us, from the consul and vice consuls to the clerks and even the cleaning ladies. One day Gisy made a vital observation. She noticed that whenever my assigned U.S. Consulate representative Leonard G. Bradford opened my folder, his attention focused on a blue document. After reviewing that blue page, he pronounced that no visa could be issued to me at this time. I pleaded that we needed the visa immediately because we were in danger of deportation. I reminded Mr. Bradford that I had fulfilled all of his previous demands for additional documentation for travel tickets and affidavits from sponsors. Mr. Bradford responded to my pleas with a sly smile and deaf ears. We were dismissed and there appeared to be no hope of receiving a visa from this bureaucrat, ever!

Many of my friends, acquaintances, and other innocent people perished because of the indifference and anti-Semitic actions taken by the staff of the American Consulate in Marseille. The anti-Semitism was not unique to the Consulate in Marseille as it represented the views of the U.S. State Department's senior leadership.[26]

During this critical time, we were incredibly lucky. Gisy's younger brother, Emil, got a job working for Mrs. Philan, who managed a relief agency that helped European intellectuals immigrate to America. Hundreds of people would wait in line each day to meet her. One of Emil's tasks for the relief agency was to visit the American Consulate and drop off documents. He could enter the Consulate without waiting in the interminable lines. Emil's easy access to the Consulate allowed Emil and his wife, Greta, to obtain U.S. visas. Emil's immigration case was handled by a different member of the Consulate staff than I had. Emil told his Consulate representative that his brother-in-law George was expecting his visa as well, and it would be desirable if we could travel together to America.

The Consulate representative did not see a problem with Emil's request, and he asked Emil to retrieve my folder from Mr. Bradford's assistant. Fortunately, Mr. Bradford was on vacation and the clerk handed my folder to Emil who proceeded up the stairs.

Emil remembered that Gisy was troubled by the presence of a blue document in my folder. Emil hid behind a pillar on the staircase where he opened my file. Inside he found the blue paper which was a copy of a telegram. The cable stated that the Karp family was being investigated by the FBI and that until the investigation was completed, Dr. Karp should be denied entry to the United States. Emil folded the page neatly and put it in his pocket. Later, when the consul inspected my folder he proclaimed that, "I do not see why these people should not have their visas." Within a few minutes, he issued our lifesaving U.S. entry visas. With these critical documents, all we needed was our French exit visas and then we would be able to travel to America! However, getting a French exit visa was very problematic.

---

26 President Roosevelt had appointed his friend Breckinridge Long to be the Assistant Secretary of State. Long sent a memo to his staff that encouraged bureaucratic delays in the immigration process. It stated that we "can delay and effectively stop for a temporary period for indefinite length the number of immigrants into the United States. We could do this by simply advising our consuls to put every obstacle in the way and to require additional evidence and to resort to various administrative devices which would postpone and postpone and postpone the granting of visas." Subak, *Rescue and Flight*, Kindle location 1437 or p. 101.

Emil and Greta Leave Marseille

NEW CHAPTER FOR SECOND EDITION WRITTEN BY LARRY BERNSTEIN

Emil and Greta Tiger aboard the Nyassa *heading from Lisbon to New York City.*

Emil and Greta left Marseille for Martinique on the *Wyoming*. Because Martinique was a French colony, refugees could depart from Marseille to the Caribbean island without a French exit visa. When a refugee arrived in Martinique, it was easy to find a boat traveling to the United States, even if the refugee lacked the requisite French exit visa.[27]

Emil's ship passage was paid for by the Austrian Socialist Party as Emil had been active in the political party before he left Vienna. The ship had an escort and traveled slowly to Casablanca, using extra caution because the previous boat out of Marseille had been torpedoed. The *Wyoming* was delayed in Casablanca, and all of its passengers were removed from the ship and detained in a camp in the Moroccan desert near Oued Zem.

When Emil lived in Marseille, he had made contacts with the American Rescue Committee (later the IRC). This relief agency was organized and managed by Varian Fry, whose office had been very helpful in assisting Emil and Greta with their various transit visas. So when Emil and Greta were detained in Morocco, I wrote to Varian Fry to use his connections and influence to assist in their release from the Moroccan camp but to no avail.[28]

Emil worked as a cook in the desert camp, and was also responsible for the camp's water rationing. Emil was respected for his efforts and his leadership in the camp and as a result was chosen to be among the first group that was released. Emil and Greta were given passage on the next ship leaving Casablanca, the *Nyassa*, for the United States and they arrived safely in New York City.

Varian Fry

27 Varian Fry describes the Martinique route. "It was the ships to Martinique which really kept us busy. We couldn't have thought up anything better if we had the power to arrange the route ourselves. They not only eliminated the trouble with the transit visas—they also removed the danger of the trip through Spain, for they went directly from Marseille to Martinique, and from there it was possible to go straight to New York." Fry, *Surrender on Demand*, 187.

Only six ships successfully made the voyage from Marseille to Martinique. See Eric Jennings, "Last Exit from Vichy France: The Martinique Escape Route and the Ambiguities of Emigration" *The Journal of Modern History*, Vol. 74, No. 2 (June 2002), 289-324. (*Photo courtesy U.S. Holocaust Museum*)

28 Varian Fry was an American whose courageous exploits helped leading European artists such as Marc Chagall, André Breton, Marcel Duchamp, Jacques Lipchitz, and Max Ernst as well as intellectuals including Hannah Arendt, Claude Levi-Strauss and Heinrich Mann escape from the Nazis. In all, Varian Fry helped over two thousand people escape France.

Our Situation Becomes Dire: November 1942

O n November 8, 1942, British and American forces invaded French North Africa and were victorious in battle. Prime Minister Winston Churchill spoke to Parliament two days later and said he had "never promised anything but blood, tears, toil, and sweat. Now, however, we have a new experience. We have victory—a remarkable and definite victory. The bright gleam has caught the helmets of our soldiers, and warmed and cheered all our hearts....Now this is not the end. It is not even the beginning of the end. But it is, perhaps, the end of the beginning."

On November 10, 1942, the German high command reciprocated by invading the unoccupied Vichy zone in southern France. There was no French opposition and the Germans marched southward. I knew it would be a matter of days before German troops reached Marseille.

The Allied war effort was improving in North Africa as well as in Stalingrad, but like other Jews in Marseille, I felt as if it was the beginning of the end.

On November 13, 1942, I witnessed the German military goose-step into Marseille. There was no time to lose. We knew the Gestapo followed the footsteps of the army within days. Although we already had our entry visas to America, we still needed our French exit visas. Getting the exit visa was not a simple process. We had to show entry visas to Spain before the exit visas could be granted. The Spanish consul did not want refugees staying in Spain so they demanded to see our American entry visas before granting us our Spanish entry visas. We also had to document to the Spanish consul that we had a transit visa to Portugal, and had paid ship passage to leave Lisbon, Portugal.

Because the Gestapo was at Marseille's doorstep we did not have time to obtain French exit visas legally. Jewish male refugees were getting arrested on sight, so it was too risky for me to walk around Marseille. Showing undiminished courage, Gisy decided to go on her own and seek out an Algerian forger known by one of our friends to prepare our fake documents. She found the forger in a bar in Marseille's *Vieux Port* and obtained our French exit visas for surprisingly little money.[29]

Although we had no passports, we had a *Sauf Conduit* issued in Marseille. We attached our American and Spanish entry visas as well as our Portuguese transit visas to the *Sauf Conduit*. With the combination of the forged French exit visa and the *Sauf Conduit*, we now had all the necessary documentation to leave France.

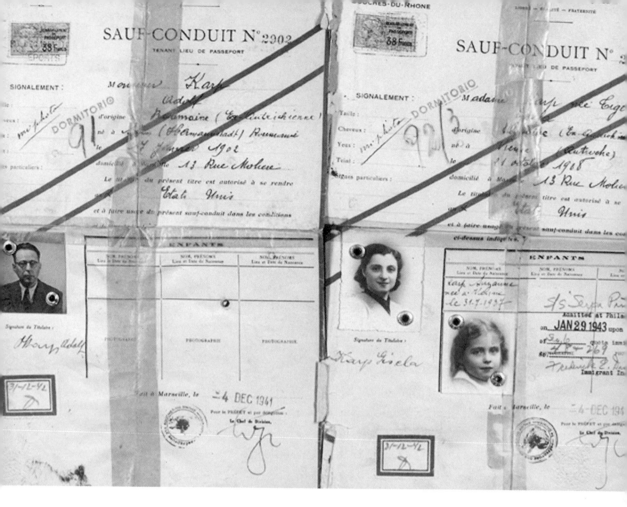

We heard rumors that the German army was already at the Spanish border, occupying the whole frontier from the east coast to the Atlantic. We had to make an escape plan, but were limited by a lack of money for transportation and supplies. When the German army marched into Marseille, all the relief agencies closed and everybody had to scramble. In this rapidly deteriorating situation, escape seemed nearly impossible.

Susie's kindergarten teacher in Mont Olivet knew of our predicament. She had a good friend at the prefecture of the police who told her that the only chance of escape was to reach the Republic of Andorra, which the Germans had not yet entered. Andorra is a very tiny country located between France and Spain. I appreciated the help but was skeptical of this plan.

Desperate, I tried to think who might be able to assist us. I had kept in touch with our former landlady in Marseille, Mme Gamel. On my visits to Marseille from Mount Olivet, I would occasionally stop at Mme Gamel's apartment. I believed that Mme Gamel was ultimately a caring woman and because she was clever, I would find some kind of help from her. She had connections with all types of people, and we trusted her counsel. We did not move from the hotel to Mount Olivet until Mme Gamel thought it advisable. Now, she gave me what I thought was our best advice under the circumstances. She told me about a female friend of hers living in Puigcerdà, a small town on France's border with Spain. The woman managed a simple bed and breakfast with a restaurant. Mme Gamel suggested that we stay there overnight, and the following day that we walk across a short bridge safely into Spain. The plan sounded simple, as only a child's dream could sound, but in spite of its risk, we decided to take her suggestion. We had spent years trying to obtain documentation to leave Marseille and come up with a good escape plan, but now we were out of time.

On the day when a number of relief agencies in Marseille closed, I went to say good-bye to my colleagues at the Jewish Agency, the Union générale des israélites de France. They gave me another document for safe conduct from Marseille, which was likely useless and was really a symbolic act of good will, for they too were at risk.

The employees of the Jewish Agency emptied the vault of all the remaining cash and distributed it among themselves. There were no long good-byes as everyone rushed out to go into hiding.

I next visited the Unitarian Service Committee where I had previously been employed. René Zimmer the medical director gave me a fine letter of recognition for my services and suggested I visit Robert Dexter who was the regional director of the organization. I met him at another hotel, where, in the most casual manner, he took out a hundred-dollar bill (a denomination rarely seen at that time) and handed it to me, thanking me for the work I had done for that committee. This $100 bill was nearly all the money we had when we left Marseille.

My next stop was to visit the Quakers. They told me that a ship would arrive in Lisbon to transport 50 Jewish children to America. My family was offered passage aboard the American bound ship, and in exchange I agreed to be responsible for the children's medical care during the voyage.

The very next day at Mont Olivet we had a lawn sale. We sold all of our belongings for very little money. The top attraction was Susie's old baby buggy. We packed a small suitcase with seemingly important items, but later we had to get rid of these possessions as well.

I learned that you can get along with practically nothing, except maybe for a toothbrush.

Every hour was dangerous, and we expected to be found and arrested. With this in mind, and encouraged by Mme Ventre, we disguised Susie as her Catholic child. Susie wore a cross around her neck, and she spoke impeccable French. She had blue eyes, blond hair, and a fair complexion that gave her an Aryan appearance. Susie easily understood that her new temporary name was Susan Ventre and she made no protest or objection, and she ably controlled her fear. Susie was not at risk as long as she was with the Ventre family.[30]

Gisy and I knew of other families who had left their children at convents or non-Jewish homes, hoping to reunite when the war was over. The Ventres told me they would have taken Susie in and treated her like their own child. I thought that our escape plan was risky and that Susie had a greater chance of survival with the Ventres. But Gisy was adamant about not leaving Susie behind and wanted to keep the family unit together at all costs. It was an emotionally tortuous decision to make, but against all odds, we chose to take our precious daughter with us. In lieu of any better option, we arranged to go together by train to the Spanish border. We had to leave immediately and follow our planned escape route. Without much explanation for Susie, we proceeded towards the St. Charles train station in Marseille. Susie did not say a word, but she looked at us and smiled. She understood and appreciated the change in plans. She communicated her happiness and contentment to me through her bright blue eyes.

---

29 Getting a legal French exit visa was extremely difficult. In the second half of 1942, only 600 Jews received valid exit visas so they could legally emigrate from Vichy France. After the American invasion of North Africa on November 8, 1942, Vichy terminated issuance of exit visas to Jews and legal emigration from France by Jews was impossible. Marrus and Paxton, *Vichy France and the Jews*, 248.

30 At this time, Jews hid their young children with Catholic institutions or foster mothers. The children assumed new names and new identities. "A child in hiding could not disclose her identity to anyone, not even to other children who could prove their Jewishness....This was no longer a game but a genuine torment....With the loss of the [child's] name, which she tried to forget so as to stay alive, she lost everything that made up her being and her memory....In a situation of such absolute solitude, lived by children so young and so ill prepared, was it possible to retain one's own identity for long? Could a child who had thus lost her points of reference ever hope to be found one day by her relatives? Can one imagine the bewilderment (in all senses of the word) that such a child must have experienced?" Samuel, *Rescuing the Children: A Holocaust Memoir*, 99.

After the war, "in thousands of homes the Jewish [child] had become so much a part of the [foster] family that separation now seemed unkind, almost impossible. Christian families begged to be allowed to keep their charges-offered to see them through school and even the university. Some even advanced the claim that by sheltering a refugee at such a risk to themselves, they had earned the right to permanent adoption; and in most cases the child in question was more than willing. But a child who became a full member of a Christian family would probably grow up Catholic or Protestant, and so be lost to the Jewish faith. Foster parents promised to avoid all pressure in this direction, but even with all possible guarantees the probability remained." Donald Lowrie, *The Hunted Children*, (Norton, 1963), 251.

Perpignan Cathedral.

Train to the Pyrenees:
November 1942

Before we left Marseille, our former landlady Mme Gamel encouraged us to make a stop in Perpignan, which is a small city in southwestern France near the Spanish border. I was to visit the local monastery and to speak only with Monseigneur X who might be able to assist us in our escape to Spain. No one else in the church was to be approached.

The trip was frightening. From the train windows, we could see the German troops marching southward. Even Susie was aware of the seriousness of the situation. Despite her age, she behaved in the most mature manner. She never cried, never asked for food, and she followed our instructions precisely.

On the train to Perpignan, we were very concerned that the French police would demand to see our travel documentation. Jews were forbidden to travel on French trains after the armistice. We told Susie that if anyone asked us any questions, she should answer. She was the only one of us who could speak French without an accent.

What we were thinking? Why would someone take the word of a child when her parents did not speak? Luckily, no one came and no questions were asked. We arrived in Perpignan without incident and exited the train station. We were frankly shocked and relieved that we were not arrested on the journey.

After receiving directions from a passerby, we went straight to the monastery. We were politely greeted by a tall, lean gentleman with short, grayish, combed back hair, who was dressed in simple priestly attire. In the most casual way, he asked what he could do for us. I told him we wanted to reach Lisbon and from there sail to America. He asked us a few questions as he tried to determine who we were. He wanted to see our papers. It was clear that this man was experienced and understandably cautious. He did not want to put himself or his church in danger.

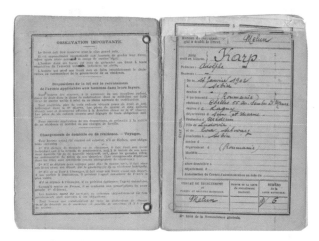

My military book with the top inch torn off.

I showed him my documents: the entry visa to America, the fake French exit visa, and my military book that noted my dismissal from the French Foreign Legion. On the front page of that book, the top one inch of the page was torn off. Monseigneur X inquired with much curiosity why that scrap had been removed and what it contained.

On the top of the page there had been a sentence in red ink, "*Ex-Autrichien engagé pour la durée de la guerre.*" The sentence translated to, "Ex-Austrian engaged for the duration of the war." The Germans condemned Austrian citizens who volunteered for the French Army. I had torn this sentence off because I was sure that if a Gestapo agent read that I had volunteered to fight the Nazis, I would be executed on the spot.[31]

With gentle prodding, Monseigneur X insisted upon knowing what had been torn off that page, but I did not tell him. Monseigneur X watched us carefully, looking at Susie repeatedly. My refusal did not make sense to him, but he clearly took a liking to us.

His dark eyes had a sharp attentive spark that expressed kindness, compassion, and an undivided attention. Even more impressive was his voice that revealed sincere interest, goodwill, and love, with natural sweetness and without artificial pretentiousness. He was pleasant and radiated friendship, and I felt like I was speaking with a close relative, a father, or an older brother.

He left for a few minutes and when he returned, he asked us to follow him to a small room with a clean tablecloth. He brought coffee for us and milk for Susie. We also received bread, butter, and chilled water. We badly needed these refreshments as we were hungry and exhausted.

After a while, he sat down close to me and said that he was not in a position to be helpful to us because the Germans were now everywhere. However, he did offer us money which I immediately refused. I erroneously believed that money was of no use to us in our present situation. He then pointed out a small station nearby where we could find a local train to Puigcerdà. We shared a warm good-bye and Monseigneur X gave me an encouraging handshake.[32]

Without further delay, we left the monastery and boarded a train that terminated in Puigcerdà. The train line served the few local residents, and we were the only foreigners aboard. There was a locomotive and two cars: one for passengers and the other for baggage. The train traveled leisurely and was not tied to any time schedule.

I was standing in the corridor of my compartment when I noticed a drunk, wearing filthy clothes, walking back and forth, talking to himself. He stopped near me and started a conversation. He wanted to know where I was traveling with my family. I confided in this stranger that we intended to sneak into Spain. He laughed with a doubtful expression, and left, only to return again with more questions. "How on earth do you figure to cross the Pyrenees Mountains and avoid the Germans who are already at the Spanish border?" He left me again and kept on swaying in a drunken manner, up and down the corridor, but he regularly returned and continued his questioning. Finally, I told him about our connections at the Puigcerdà restaurant.

When the drunk returned for the last time, he said in a clear and sober voice, "I hope you will succeed with your plan, but if you have difficulties, you can find me in the town's restaurant bar every day. I will help you." Without waiting for my reaction, he stumbled away and disappeared.

After passing a few stations without incident, the train stopped, and the conductor announced that all passengers were to leave their luggage, and disembark to have their traveling documents examined. All the French travelers aboard had papers for this purpose as they took this train daily. Our compartment emptied of its handful of French women. We decided not to leave our train compartment, and we sat frozen in our seats. We did not speak and pretended to sleep. Susie was calm and collected and did not draw any attention; she knew her role. In a short while, the passengers returned, and the train started again. We never knew whether no one noticed that we did not disembark or whether we were ignored due to someone's benevolent intervention.[33]

The restaurant in Puigcerdà was easy to find because it was the only one in town. We heard German conversations and shouting when we arrived at the restaurant. We knew it was dangerous to enter but we had no alternative because there was nowhere else to go.

Our former landlady in Marseille, Mme Gamel told us that our contact would be the woman managing this restaurant. Our hope was that she could help and guide us across the Spanish border.

The small restaurant had a few rooms for rent. We got a room and waited for an opportunity to speak with her in private, which was not easy as she was the only person working outside of the kitchen. She did everything except cook; she rented rooms and served food and drinks in the restaurant and bar.

The restaurant was packed with German soldiers who were eating and drinking. Most of them appeared to be officers, and several orderlies were running back and forth to the kitchen. All this was done with military order, with continuous, "*Jawohl, Herr Kommandant.*" They stood at attention, saluted, and clicked their heels, with boots that shined like mirrors. We were lucky that this was an advance army unit that did not care about Jewish refugees. The Gestapo was not here yet, and the soldiers paid no attention to us. I assume that it did not occur to them to find Jews here, practically in the lion's mouth.

German soldiers surrounded us and were in the adjacent hotel rooms and in the restaurant and kitchen below. They were all over the place. In Vienna, while the Nazis were omnipresent, we could hide in a big city. In Marseille we were even safer. In Mont Olivet, I never saw a single German soldier. But here in Puigcerdà, we were in serious danger as soldiers were everywhere.

The German Army unit's close proximity was shattering to us, and the sound of the German voices was a paralyzing blow. The arrogant commands and the self-confident shouting from the restaurant were almost too much to endure. When we got ready for bed, we could hear two German officers conversing from our adjacent hotel room. That night I had my first nightmare. I dreamt that we had been captured and transported east to a German concentration camp. Gisy woke me to stop my screaming. Fortunately, our neighbors were sleeping soundly after enjoying a good French meal served with plenty of red wine.

I got up early the following morning and found our contact in the restaurant.

She had read Mme Gamel's letter, so she knew who we were and what we wanted from her. Unfortunately, Germans were now guarding the small, wooden border bridge that we had planned to walk across to freedom. There was nothing she could do for us. Our naive and childish dream could not be realized.

Now we were stuck.

At least in Marseille, Susie could disguise herself as a Catholic girl with a cross around her neck and the Ventres family would have been able to protect her. But now, we were all at risk. Our scheme had been a complete failure and we had no backup plan. We were desperate, and we feared for the worst.

---

31 This concern was justified because of German General Keitel's "infamous 'Night and Fog' order of December 7, 1941. This order decreed the instant execution of all non-German civilians found guilty of 'criminal acts against the Reich or the occupation authorities'....Beyond the mere announcement of their arrest, no news about the fate of such deportees would be provided-hence the name 'Night and Fog.' From the names of the victims on reprisal execution lists, it was obvious that a large number of Jews were being included." Claude Chambard, *The Maquis: A History of the French Resistance Movement*, (Macmillan General Reference, 1976), 28.

32 Editor's note: the author never explains why he refers to the priest only as Monseigneur X. It might have been Henri-Marius Bernard who was the Monseigneur of Perpignan from 1933-1959.

33 Just a few days prior to our leaving Marseille, on November 9, 1942, Vichy passed a law that forbade Jews "to move freely from place to place or leave their commune of residence without police authorization," which was to be granted only sparingly. Marrus and Paxton, *Vichy France and the Jews*, 304.

The Maquis Connection: November 1942

The next morning, I was the first and only patron in the restaurant and there were no German soldiers present at this early hour. I hunched over my coffee, completely despondent. To my surprise, "the drunk" from the train entered the café and signaled for me to join him. Given my predicament, there was nothing to lose by talking with him. I told the drunk that my connection was of no help, and he said without looking up from his glass of wine in a very authoritative tone, "Listen carefully."

"Take the next local train to a nearby town. It leaves in half an hour, so do not waste any time. After you arrive, go directly to a bistro that is across from the station. You have to be careful. The Germans are not there yet, but the French local police are loyal to Pétain."

The so-called drunk continued in a surprisingly clear way. "Do not smoke or even strike a match, and do not move around so no one will suspect you are there. As long as you stay in that village bistro, no one will bother you. Wait there for a man. Follow his directions and do exactly as you are told. We have arranged for your family to go to Spain, but you will have to cross the Pyrenees Mountains on foot." After he finished speaking, he stood and said, "I will not say *au revoir*, because you will not see me again." Then he left the restaurant.

I persuaded Gisy to follow his instructions and we hurried to the station. The train leaving Puigcerdà was an old, pre-WWI vintage, with a coal-driven locomotive followed by a baggage car. We were the only passengers on the train along with the engineer and the conductor. My last little piece of luggage was stolen from me on that train. The conductor was the likely thief. He correctly assumed that he could take what he wanted and no one would ask questions. I did not look for the bag, and we proceeded directly to the bistro.

The little town was deserted. We found the bistro easily, and we entered through the unlocked door. The place seemed abandoned and the shelves were bare. We made ourselves comfortable around a table. Gisy was especially restless as she did not trust the "drunk." I was confused, to put it mildly. I did not know who or what to believe, but I decided to follow the drunk's plan, whatever the outcome. In any case, I could see no alternative. To turn back to the interior of France and hide was unthinkable. To proceed across the border also seemed impossible. To make matters worse, it was also certain that the Germans would arrive in this village imminently.

The ghostly town was soothing in a strange way, but it did not give us comfort.

We waited impatiently for an unknown man to lead us to safety. Darkness fell and no lights went on in the streets. The houses were dark, and the town remained uninhabited. We were hungry, but this was not one of our primary concerns. Gisy always had some food for Susie, and as long as our child was satisfied, we were content.

As we were preparing for sleep, we saw in the distance a tall man walking toward the bistro. It was not possible to distinguish between a policeman, a soldier, or a friend. A tall man entered the bistro and told us to follow him. He waved off my questions and motioned to me not to speak. We left together and walked at a brisk pace for over an hour until we were far out of town.

Our guide walked in a deliberate manner and it seemed the route was well known to him. In the dim, moonlit sky, we could see the menacing heights of the Pyrenees. These tall mountains appeared so close to us that it seemed we could reach out and touch them. Our apprehension mounted.

Now that we were outside of the village, we could talk freely. The man introduced himself as Armand and informed us that he was a member of the Maquis, which he explained was a loose organization made up of predominantly rural, French armed resistance fighters. The French word "Maquis" refers to the Corsican underbrush, which is known as an excellent hiding place for outlaws.[34]

Armand informed us that we would be temporarily residing in an abandoned farmhouse in the countryside. A neighboring farmer tended his fields just 200 feet away. The farmer was not to be approached because he was a Pétain loyalist and was undoubtedly dangerous.

Armand explained that our stay at this farmhouse would probably last for many days and that we were to wait for the right opportunity to depart to Spain. We were hungry and had not eaten all day, so Armand promised to return with food before daylight.

Maquis fighters (courtesy US Holocaust Museum).

The old farmhouse had a large bedroom and a small kitchen with a stove and plenty of cut wood, but Armand prohibited us from making a fire because the smoke would give us away. During the day, we were not allowed to go outside, and we felt like prisoners.

After Armand left us, we groped around in the dark to find a place to lie down, and we immediately went to sleep. Our fatigue overcame danger, anxiety, and hunger. We slept soundly until just before sunrise when we were awakened by Armand's knock on the door. He brought us cold food for several days including fresh boiled eggs, bread, cheese, and some meat as well as milk for Susie. In the kitchen there was a large sink with a cold water faucet and a towel. We suddenly felt quite happy.

Armand's early morning visits developed into a routine. He would appear daily before sunrise with the same care package. He did not know how long we would stay at the farmhouse. However, he did give us hope that we would leave soon.

We faced additional adversities. It was now November, and while the weather was mild and sunny in the valley, we worried about the cold and snow on top of the mountains. We were physically unprepared for these conditions, but we had no choice and had to face them. When we left Marseille, our intent was to cross the border into Spain by walking over a wooden bridge, and therefore we did not have gear for mountain climbing. In particular, Gisy had only a pair of high-heeled shoes that were completely unsuitable for the journey ahead. We discussed the issue with Armand, and while he too was concerned, he doubted he could find Gisy proper footwear.

The first few days passed. From our closed windows, we watched the neighboring farmer tend his fields alone; obviously his family was gone. The farmer was unaware of our presence in the farmhouse, and he paid no attention to the beautiful Pyrenees surrounding him.

We stared in awe at the high mountain just 300 yards in front us. We were baffled as to how Susie would manage to climb the mountain. Whenever Armand visited us, we spoke about our fears, but he assured us that we could all manage the climb.

Several days passed. Despite our inactivity, we were not bored; we were emotionally overwhelmed by the seemingly impossible task ahead. Gisy quickly lost confidence in the whole enterprise and considered Armand's plan foolhardy. I disagreed with her, and we had heated discussions, which filled our days of waiting.

One night the familiar knock sounded at the door around midnight instead of the usual time around sunrise. I opened the door and saw fear on Gisy's face. Armand asked me to follow him immediately and to bring all of our money. Gisy became hysterical. She feared that I would be robbed and killed, and she would be left completely alone with Susie. An angry discussion in German ensued between us. Armand got impatient because there was no time to waste. Even though I was unsuccessful in reassuring Gisy, I left with Armand.

I was scared, but I followed Armand into a dense forest. As we walked, I was worried that the Maquis might refuse to let us participate in the mountain escape. It was risky to include our family in the plan: a woman without proper shoes, a five-year-old child, and a man no longer of fighting age.

It was very quiet except for the sound of Armand's sure and confident steps. Armand walked through the forest in a straight and clear way despite the darkness, until we reached a clearing.

It was pitch black; I could not see anything at all. We stopped and Armand spoke in a low voice to someone else. I was tense and full of anticipation, but peculiarly not anxious. I knew this was one of those turning points in life, and I felt a sort of fatalistic calm take hold of me, some kind of narcotic mixture of fear and confidence.

Suddenly, I was blinded by a bright flashlight, pointed in my face at close range. When I regained my sight, I discovered that I was surrounded by a group of armed men with revolvers at their hips. I was very frightened but tried to concentrate and assess the situation. These men were dressed in ordinary work clothes, and each of them wore a dark beret—not the kind of beret used by elite units of the French army—but berets more typically worn by local Basque shepherds. Based on Armand's previous comments, I quickly surmised that I had joined a meeting of the Maquis.

The apparent leader of the group was a stocky Frenchman who spoke in a commanding and intellectual manner. "*Monsieur*," he said to me, "Monseigneur X told us about you. We are aware of your enlistment with the French Foreign Legion and that you have a wife and child. Our primary mission is to rescue English fliers who were shot down in France. We help British pilots flee from the Germans and return to England. We rarely make exceptions and help refugees, but in your case, because of your readiness to serve France by joining the French Foreign Legion, we will help you. Our operation is expensive, and our funds are limited. It is therefore necessary that we get money from everyone who is not on active military duty. I must ask you to hand over all of your money."

I gave him 150 francs and 50 U.S. dollars, which was all the money that I had. He was clearly disappointed. For some reason, he thought I had a lot more money, and he told me so. When I assured him that my wife had only small change in her purse, he acknowledged my explanation with a nod and dismissed me saying, "We will take care of you."[35]

To my surprise, I noticed that seated among us was the "drunk" whom I had met on the train. I now understood that he had been my Maquis contact all along.[36]

The flashlight was turned off, and we were again in pitch darkness. Armand took my hand and walked me home. On the way, he told me that we would leave the next night. I suddenly was overjoyed. I felt that my family was going to be saved from sure destruction and that I was ready to follow Armand and the Maquis anywhere. With my new found hope, I had a renewed sense of strength and courage, and I knew that I had to transfer that feeling to Gisy.

When we arrived back at the farmhouse, Gisy was visibly relieved. She had been sure that she would never see me again.

That night, Gisy and I could not sleep. The few days we had spent in the farmhouse had given us a sense of security. Now, the Pyrenees Mountains, which were literally directly in front of us, cast a dark shadow with unknown threats and dangers. I told Gisy all about the discussions with the Maquis, and tried my best to instill confidence about the journey ahead. Gisy had her own strength. It was a wonderful gift of hers that we all relied on; without it, we could never have made it this far.

As promised, the following night Armand picked us up and we started walking. Armand handed Gisy a pair of hand woven espadrilles that had multilayered cord soles. These shoes fit Gisy's feet poorly, were uncomfortable and were not sturdy, but they would be better than high heels to climb the mountains. Armand forbade us from taking anything, and so we left with only the clothes on our back. Gisy filled her pockets with cubes of sugar from our breakfast table, and I put some breadcrumbs and a dried piece of cheese in my pocket. After waking, Susie shook off her sleepiness and was alert and cooperative. And we were off.

We returned to that little village with the bistro where we had first arrived by train days before. We entered a small bakery that had an open pit. A fire was burning and a man with a long wooden shovel was removing bread, which filled the room with a mouth-watering aroma. Shortly thereafter, we were served our first hot meal in weeks. I do not remember what we ate, but I will never forget the red wine. There is no way to tell whether it was the circumstances or the quality, but the taste was so delicious that it made a lasting impression on me. No wine since has tasted that good.

Several people entered the bakery and no one paid us any attention. Then three policemen arrived to our consternation. I had the distinct impression that they looked us over very carefully. After some freshly baked bread was brought to them, they left. We waited a long time before departing, and Susie fell asleep in Gisy's lap.

---

34 Early in 1941, scattered anti-German groups emerged in France, particularly after young French men were relocated and forced to work in German labor camps. Helped by their English allies who air-dropped munitions, these French guerillas sabotaged railroads and power plants. Their ambush of German troops often led to savage German reprisals against local French civilians.

The members of the Maquis believed that France should be led by General de Gaulle instead of the current leader of Vichy France, Marshal Pétain, who they believed was a collaborator and a traitor. Charles de Gaulle managed the French resistance from London. In his declaration on June 23, 1942, de Gaulle denounced Pétain and said "It is the sacred duty of every man to contribute all he can to the liberation of our country through the invader's defeat....Yet this gigantic ordeal has shown the nation that the danger threatening its existence does not come solely from outside, and that victory without courageous and thorough internal reconstruction would not be real victory." The "economic régime, paralyzed by corruption, has abdicated in defeat. Another, arising from a criminal capitulation, is drunk with personal power. Both are condemned by the French people who, even as they unite for victory, are massing for revolution."

35 After the Germans invaded Vichy France in November 1942, an estimated 30,000 mostly Jewish refugees tried to cross the Spanish border illegally. "Local guides took the people across, and to the hazards of police and border guards were added the hazard of fraud and robbery by some unscrupulous opportunists. Up to 50,000 francs were demanded for passage into Spain." Marrus and Paxton, *Vichy France and the Jews*, 309.

36 Editor's note: Anonymity was a structural necessity for clandestine subversive activities. The author did not know the name of the Maquis leader but we suspect it was Ernest Zaugg who was the Maquis leader in the Querigut-Rouze-Miganès-Roc-Blanc sector. His alias was "Le Sanglier" which translates to "wild boar." Some of the Maquis went by their first name; others were given a *nom de guerre*. Zaugg, who was previously employed as a hydro-electric engineer, focused on managing an escape route to Spain. He organized two camps near Roc Blanc in the Pyrenees. The Maquis leaders were not appointed but instead were chosen organically around an individual who was dynamic, smart, articulate, and careful. Kedward, *In Search of the Maquis: Rural Resistance in Southern France 1942-1944*, Clarendon Press, 1995, 32, 46, 91, 252 and 258.

See also http://audealaculture.fr/sites/default/files/Archives/resistance_et_clandestinite.pdf

Climbing the Pyrenees:
Late November 1942

After dark, Armand informed us that it was time to leave. We exited the bakery and walked briskly to the base of the mountain. We observed that the ascent was going to be very steep. After waiting a few minutes, we were joined by a portly, middle-aged man who previously worked as an attorney for the British consul in Marseille. In addition, the consul for the Polish embassy arrived with his wife. Our group now comprised five adults and Susie.

While we waited in the dark, Armand suddenly walked away, leaving us alone. We were confused and frightened as we huddled in the pitch black in an unfamiliar location. The two other men conversed in an excited manner in a language that I could not decipher.

We had no choice but to wait for our guide. To make our situation worse, it started to drizzle. The night was not cold, but the wetness and the slight wind and the closeness of the mountain were disquieting. The reality of our task was beginning to set in. We would have to cross this forbidding mountain on foot, with no shelter, no matter the weather: cold, rain, or snow.

We never saw Armand again.

A few minutes later, our new guide, Manuel, introduced himself, and he told us that he would bring us to Spain. He was immediately joined by a large group of British pilots and a couple of other refugees. These twenty-year-old Brits had been shot down over France and were being rescued by the Maquis. The pilots hoped to return to England to continue the fight against the Germans.

Our guide signaled to us to follow him and within minutes we were climbing. We slowed down when we reached a wooden bridge that was slightly submerged by ankle-high running water. The structure's purpose was to divert water from a nearby small creek to the fields. It was not intended for people to cross, and our guide chose

this path precisely because no one would suspect people of using it to navigate the stream. We struggled across the bridge and kept on walking at a brisk pace. The drizzle did not abate and our feet were wet and cold. Then, the climb got steeper.

Gisy and I had difficulty keeping up with the fast-moving group because we had to assist Susie. In no time at all, we were alone. Our distance from the group kept widening but shouting ahead was dangerous.

Finally we stopped in the complete darkness. No moon favored us, and we could not see a pathway to follow. As we climbed, we'd been walking on grass, then between bushes and boulders, but not on paths used by people. Under these circumstances, it was inadvisable to move ahead on our own, so we waited and hoped that our guide would find us. The drizzle intensified to a hard rain, and it felt like an eternity, but in reality, we did not have to wait long. Manuel reappeared from nowhere. It seemed a miracle that he found us in the dark.

Our guide Manuel was a Spanish smuggler, and he was very familiar with this terrain, since he covered these tracks several times a year. He appeared to be around thirty-five years of age, a muscular and strong man with weathered skin, a dark, rugged complexion and a friendly demeanor. It became immediately evident that he was a very intelligent, attentive man, with good judgment. He properly sized up each member of the group. I felt complete confidence in his ability to lead us to safety, and in his goodwill to do so.

After finding us, the group walked at a slower pace. I suspect that it was partly in consideration for us and partly due to the steadily increasing slope. Manuel occasionally took Susie in his arms to facilitate our ascent. We continued climbing for hours until we reached a mountain top. The temperatures dropped at the higher altitudes, and we were now cold, wet, and tired.

On top of that first mountain, Manuel led us to a small cave. A few of us entered, and it was a relief to get out of the rain. Gisy in particular, with her string shoes, was soaked to the bone. She was anxious to remove her shoes and to dry her feet.

There was room for only a few of us in the tiny cave. Obviously there was no door or window and we did not expect to find a fireplace. Our guide made a fire with wet and dry branches that emitted a heavy smoke that burned our eyes and made us choke. However, we appreciated the heat and dried ourselves. Although it was unpleasant, we had to warm up. After the worst of the smoke abated, we lay down on the bare earth and slept for a few hours. The following morning, we were greeted with wonderful weather. The sun was warm and the drizzle had given way to clean, dry air.

I had never been so closely surrounded by so many mountains. I had grown up in Sibiu near the beautiful Carpathian Mountains where I often hiked. In fact, our family name, Karp, derives from the German spelling of Carpathian. On our honeymoon, Gisy and I traveled to the Austrian Alps around Innsbruck. However, I had never before seen those mountains from the heights that I now saw the Pyrenees. It was alarming to see the surrounding peaks because I knew we had to climb them to reach Spain. Nonetheless, I marveled at the beauty of this majestic scenery with crystal-clear creeks running down at stunning speeds from snow-capped mountains. We drank the delicious cold water using our cupped hands. Thank goodness, we were able to avoid the most forbidding heights because of our guide's local knowledge.

On this glorious morning, we were confronted by the British flyers who were angry that we were slowing them down. They claimed that the child's presence added additional risks to the journey. But there was nothing the Brits could do because Manuel refused to be intimidated by them. Our guide earned everyone's respect and obedience.

Gisy, with her cord espadrilles, had a very hard time mountain climbing. When her shoes got wet, they rubbed her feet raw which was incredibly painful, and I was worried that her open sores could lead to infection. One of the other refugees had a pair of brand-new boots wrapped around his neck, while the pair he was wearing was also in excellent condition. In vain, I begged him to lend Gisy his extra pair of shoes. He simply said, "I did not bring these shoes all this way to have her wear them." I asked if he would loan them to my wife for the time being, and as soon as he needed them, we would return them. He curtly refused. In all my life, I have never encountered such a selfish and unkind person.

Days later, when nobody had eaten for more than two days, the man with the extra pair of boots did not hesitate to ask Gisy for a sugar cube that she had brought for Susie. We gave some to him and to the others as well. Later, he asked me "do you know who I am?" I answered that I didn't know and that I didn't care. Today, I regret not asking him for his name, because I would like to know who that SOB was.

The valley before us was covered with short, coarse grass and cacti, which were painful to walk on, but our guide led us forward. The day was pleasant and filled with sunshine. One of the tall, blond, English flyers occasionally carried Susie to speed things up. He told me, in strict confidence that all of them were armed and, in the event that we ran into German or Spanish patrols, that they would shoot to kill. He told me this, not to scare us, but so that we would be prepared to look for cover and to protect Susie.

We had no problems walking down the mountain. The valley looked deserted, and we saw nothing on the horizon. When we arrived at the next mountain, we had a much steeper ascent. The pace of our climb was too fast for me, yet the flyers urged us to keep pace. I gradually became short of breath, had palpitations, and knew that if I did not slow down, I would be in serious trouble. I sat down among the cacti and let the group march on. I knew that our guide, Manuel, would soon discover my absence and return for me. He stopped the group, came back, and ordered a well-deserved five minute rest for all of us, despite the flyers' protest.

We started climbing again, and the mountain became steeper, which slowed us down. We followed barely visible paths on the side of the mountain. We often saw bones, some human, others animal, but we never stopped to examine them.

The trail was dangerous and we had to grab onto thorny branches and rocks to prevent us from falling and rolling down the mountain. Gisy was in the worst shape. Because of her rope shoes, it was very difficult for her to walk, and it was necessary for her to hold onto prickly branches for support. In no time, her hands were bleeding because of the sharp barbs.

Susie was very cooperative throughout this difficult time, and she observed everything with her blue eyes. Susie acted calmly and appropriately without complaint or crying, and she exhibited a more mature attitude than most children twice her age. Once, after Manuel noticed a patrol in the distance, he signaled to us to hide behind a mound. We all ducked, and Susie automatically did the same. She sensed intuitively that we were in dire circumstances, and she made all the necessary adjustments with amazing speed and precision.

We climbed and descended several mountain ranges, some in a serpentine fashion and others directly. We climbed for days, mostly in the early morning or in the late evening. We were exhausted and climbed slower than before, but we kept climbing. We were all completely drained from the constant movement, and terribly hungry; even the more fit British pilots showed fatigue.

Eventually, Manuel signaled us to halt. It was twilight and there was still good visibility. We could see that the top of the mountain was not far away, and he directed us to a small area where we huddled together. We waited until after dark before moving again. After climbing for an hour or more, we saw a few lights flickering from a small village in the distance. It was a bright night, so we had to proceed in complete silence. Manuel was in front, and we followed slowly in single file. We approached the town from the back, which was encircled by a five-foot-high, broken down wall. Manuel signaled to us to wait. He disappeared into an opening in the wall, which was made by removing some of the bricks. Manuel returned a few minutes later and motioned to follow him through the wall opening.

Manuel led us to an old barn that contained a few cows and some other farm animals. In silence, we climbed the ladder attached to the side of the building that took us to the barn's loft. The barn stank. After our eyes got used to the darkness, we looked out the loft's three tiny windows, and saw an amazing sight: a small town at this high altitude. We admired the houses receding all the way down the mountain.

Close by were the neighbors' farms, and we could hear the sound of chickens and sheep but conspicuously absent was the sound of dogs barking. I suspect that there were probably no dogs because, had there been, they would have alerted outsiders to the arrival of strangers. Our farmhouse was dark and camouflaged in the night. It seemed obvious that the barn had previously been used for centuries to accommodate fugitives like us. I wondered if those seeking shelter here were political refugees or criminals on the run. Did they travel from France to Spain or vice versa? The local chief of police must surely have known about this hiding place.

Manuel reappeared with a dim kerosene lamp that spread a ghostly shadow. The Polish consul had a rudimentary knowledge of Spanish and the two spoke quietly. The consul informed us that the farmer's wife could slaughter a lamb and prepare us a stew for a fee. Most of us had no money to pay her, but we were all extremely hungry. The last warm meal we had was at the bakery. The fat British attorney announced that he would pay for the stew for all of us.

The barn loft's floor had a simple row of planks supported by wooden beams. The planks were reasonably clean, and in no time at all, we were asleep. Later, when the steaming hot, aromatic dish arrived, I could not wake either Gisy or Susie, despite heavy prodding. Both of them slept soundly until late the next morning. By then, all the stew had been devoured and not a morsel remained for them to eat. They received some goat's milk and bread in the morning, which was all they had to eat until the following night.

The meal had a transformative effect on the group. The prospect of alleviating our severe hunger did wonders for morale. Everyone became relaxed, friendly, and even pleasant. The British pilots started their first real conversation with the rest of us. Despite the poor light from the kerosene lamp, I could see all the haggard faces with wide smiles. It was a happy moment and the food had done wonders for everyone's demeanor.

We stayed in the barn all day. It was now late November and the temperature was cool but tolerable under the flimsy roof. We passed our time looking through the three windows, observing the farmers tending their livestock. I saw some children with their books heading to the school that was located at the edge of the town. A small church was visible and we could hear the soothing sound of the bell during the day. It seemed bizarre to find a functioning town at this altitude, and to see such colorful, winding streets, surrounded by cultivated fields.

We left the farm after dark. We circled around the outside of town and our guide, with his customary skill, easily found the way for our descent. It continually amazed me that Manuel was able to find his way in complete darkness.

The way down the mountain was relatively easy, but to make certain of our safety, Manuel had to follow a winding route, which took nearly all night. We arrived before sunrise at the bottom of the Pyrenees, deep inside Spanish territory.

We were stunned when Manuel informed us that his mission with us ended here. From now on, we were to proceed without his guidance. It was dark; there was no moonlight or even a flicker from an electric light anywhere to assist us. Manuel sensed our alarm. He explained that although he would like to help us farther, it was too dangerous for him to do so. Over the past few years, he had helped hundreds of people escape the authorities in both directions across the border. We presumed that he had also been active with the Spanish Republican Army during the Spanish civil war and had good reason to avoid the fascist Spanish authorities. Although we feared to proceed without him, we understood that Manuel's safety depended on his hiding in the shadows of the Pyrenees. The mountains were his permanent home, his source of life.

Manuel handed a compass to one of the British flyers and explained how to reach the local train station that would take us to Barcelona. With much trepidation and regret, we parted and walked in the direction Manuel had indicated.

Spain and Portugal: November 1942

After Manuel left, the British pilots promptly abandoned us, leaving us alone in the dark without a compass. The rest of us—Gisy, Susie, the fat British lawyer, the Polish couple, and I—walked aimlessly for nearly half an hour. No town was near. There was no light or gas lamp in the area to assist us. We were like a group of blind people groping around without a cane. And then suddenly, there was much commotion, and we were surrounded by Spanish soldiers pointing their guns and bayonets at us. We were their prisoners.

The soldiers led us to a military camp and into an interrogation room that was lit by a single electric bulb, dangling from the ceiling by a cord. The room was sparsely furnished with only a worn, unvarnished table, and one chair for the five of us. A young officer entered and inspected us with obvious curiosity. He noticed Susie first, then looked at the British attorney and the Polish couple, and finally at me. Then he asked in a most serious, threatening voice, "Where are the others?" He spoke in French so we could easily communicate.

I pretended not to understand his question. The officer then told me he had received a report that other people were with us. He wanted to know who these others were and where they had gone. I told him that our group consisted solely of the Polish consul and his wife, the British attorney, plus the three members of my family. I got the impression that he did not believe my answer, but he moved on. He asked us why we had entered Spanish territory and what our intended plans were in Spain. Now, the attorney spoke up. He explained that we were fleeing from the Germans and that our goal was to reach Lisbon, Portugal. The attorney and the Polish couple wished to proceed subsequently to London. I informed the officer that we already had paid passage on a ship sailing from Lisbon to our destination in the United States.

The officer became noticeably relieved once he understood that we were not seeking refuge in Spain. He demanded that we place all of our possessions on the table including our passports and visas. We all complied and emptied our pockets. The fat British attorney took off his jacket, then his vest, and unwound a wide cloth that was closely fitted around his abdomen. After taking the contraption off, he placed it on the table and emptied the double-lined pocket that was full of dollars and English pounds. There was now a mountain of money on the table, and we were all as astonished as the officer.

After inspecting our papers, the officer handed them back to us and exited into another room. After a brief telephone conversation, he returned with a smile and spoke to us in a pleasant way. He wanted to know how long we had been on our journey and seemed dumbfounded that we had traveled so many miles, with a little girl, on such an arduous trip over the Pyrenees. When we told him that we were hungry, he ordered us food with milk and chocolate for Susie.

This very kind officer possessed traditional Spanish courtesy and couldn't seem to do enough for our child. To our surprise, he returned our belongings, including all the money to the now not-so-fat attorney.

The officer explained that, under a Spanish-German agreement, illegal entrants to Spain captured within 250 miles of the French border had to be returned to Germany. We had been arrested within that zone; however, he admitted that the military command did not always follow this official policy. Since we all had Portuguese transit visas, he would not detain us further.

Our group of refugees was not a threat. Had they captured the armed British pilots instead, the Spanish authorities probably would have returned them to Germany. The objective of the Spanish-German agreement was to prevent the escape of Allied hostile combatants from France.

The officer ordered a military escort to take us to the train station. After the two Spanish soldiers left us there, we stayed patiently in the tiny station's waiting room. Our British pilots rejoined us at the station moments before we all boarded the train to Barcelona.

When we arrived at our destination, we all went our separate ways. It was inadvisable to stay together as a group. We all had worn the same clothing for the past few weeks and would stand out, so it was best to split up and not attract the local police.

I found a small hotel with a clean room and bath for my family. With her swollen feet and bandaged hands, Gisy immediately went to sleep. She was completely exhausted and had reached her physical limit. For the next three days, Gisy did not move from her bed. After she woke, the pain and swelling in her hands and feet remained.

Since we entered Spain illegally, we did not have the proper Spanish entry stamp affixed to our passports. Therefore, our first matter of business in Barcelona was to get our papers in order. After paying a fine for our unlawful border crossing, we received official documentation that we had entered Spain.

I then contacted a local affiliate of the same Jewish relief agency that had employed me in Marseille. After reviewing my credentials, the agency immediately provided us with monetary assistance.

When I was in the waiting room at the Jewish agency, you would never believe who walked in. It was my fellow mountain climber with the extra pair of shoes around his neck. Our eyes locked and then I looked down at his feet and noticed he was wearing the extra boots! I looked at him with contempt and he left in a hurry. I deeply regret not getting his name so I could inform the world of this truly wretched human being.

In any case, with the money I had received, I immediately went to a nearby store and purchased my wife a new pair of comfortable shoes.

The Jewish agency also provided us train tickets from Barcelona to the Portuguese border, which was an incomplete itinerary to Lisbon. An official from the Barcelona Jewish relief agency told me that a local representative would meet us at the Portuguese border. This travel arrangement seemed idiotic, but I had no recourse.

Our overnight train across Spain was packed and we arrived the following morning on November 22, 1942 at the Portuguese border station. On arrival, we could not find our contact from the Jewish Agency at the prearranged location. We were desperate because we had no money to purchase a train ticket to Lisbon.

As we walked back and forth on the train platform, trying to find our contact, a local man overheard our German conversation and saw that we were panicked. After learning about our predicament, he purchased the train tickets to Lisbon for us. Our rescuer's name was José Manuel la Costa, a linguistics professor at the University of Madrid. We developed a friendly relationship with him and, of course, repaid our debt as soon as we were able.

The train to Lisbon was nearly empty when we departed the border station. It made local stops, and soon the train compartment was full, so people were forced to stand in the aisle. Susie and I gave up our seats to two German-speaking women. Gisy conversed with them, and by the time we arrived in Lisbon, we had gratefully accepted an invitation to spend the night at one of their homes. The following day, we visited the Jewish Agency's Lisbon office, and they provided us money for a decent small hotel.

Lisbon, November 28, 1942

Dearest Sophie,

Because we haven't heard from you, we don't know if you received our telegram informing you of our safe arrival in Lisbon. It is a miracle, but under what severe circumstances!

Our only way to leave France and get to Spain was to climb the Pyrenees. We struggled for three nights, making dangerous progress over stony terrain. During the days we hid in the woods or in caves.

We arrived in Spain in appalling condition. We had to leave all of our possessions behind, even the most important. Otherwise, we couldn't have made it.

On the train to Lisbon, we met a family that offered to take us in, and they helped us in so many ways. Right away on the first day, we bought underwear for Susie. Then we borrowed their underwear so that we could wash ours. And they continue to help us.

At this time there are no ships leaving Lisbon to take us anywhere. We will probably have to stay here until at least the end of December. By that time, we should be in somewhat better condition to travel. George and I have lost a lot of weight. Despite all the traumatic experiences, Susie looks relatively well and has grown a lot.

It is unimaginable what a child can take. She ran so many kilometers without protesting.

Susie and Dita.

Susie understood that she could not make a sound and had to hide. She never complained about being hungry despite days without food. Thank God, she looks well.

On the first evening of our climb, perhaps due to the exhaustion, Susie suddenly developed a high fever. George and I were alarmed by this. But the next morning she was fine and continued on the escape.

Our new friends in Lisbon are in love with our child and sometimes say, "Susie, will you stay with us when your parents go to America?" But Susie always answers the same way, "I go to my Dita." Sophie, she can't wait to see your daughter, Dita.

Hopefully no additional obstacles will delay our travels.

When we arrived in Lisbon, I sent a telegram to mother; I wonder if she received it? How is our dear mother? Will I ever see her again? How glad she must be that we are no longer trapped in Marseille.

In Lisbon, the stores are full and there are still so many good things to eat. Our eyes popped when we saw such choice and abundance. George got an upset stomach from eating too much, and I am bursting as well. We can only eat the smallest of portions, but I am sure that we will learn how to eat again.

Please write soon and give our warmest greetings to all.

Your Gisy

Saving Jewish Orphans: Late 1942
NEW CHAPTER FOR REVISED EDITION WRITTEN BY LARRY BERNSTEIN

I n August 1942, Vichy France sent thousands of French and foreign Jews to the concentration camps in the East. Donald Lowrie, an American working for the relief agencies in Marseille, pressed Marshal Pétain and his minister, Pierre Laval, to let 50 Jewish children immigrate to America.[37] Laval demanded that if the United States would take 50 Jewish children, then why not take them all? The local relief agencies successfully persuaded Admiral Leahy, the U.S. ambassador to Vichy, and U.S. Secretary of State Cordell Hull, to provide entry visas for 5,000 Jewish children.[38]

Child inmates of the Rivesaltes Internment Camp, in Vichy, France (courtesy US Holocaust Museum).

After his demands were met, Laval then became concerned about the American public reaction to the French policy of splitting up families. He suspected that when the Jewish children arrived in New York, Mayor LaGuardia would use it as a pretext for an anti-Vichy speech.[39] So the U.S. government acquiesced to Laval and promised that there would be no public ceremonies with the Jewish children.

The relief agencies let it be known that the children would be given U.S. visas and requested volunteers. Dr. Joseph Weill who worked at the Jewish Children's Aid Society and at the Marseille medical clinic detailed what a separation was like. "At the moment of separation, the parents proved to be of admirable dignity and calm. Almost all of them informed us of their last wishes, handed their jewels and clothes over to their children, and often expressed their wishes as to their education and future. Many of them blessed their children with a biblical phrase. They asked them to be courageous, worthy of their Jewishness, and not to forget them. And with an abrupt gesture, they turned around to hide their emotion. Not one of these mothers went back to their children."[40] No one will ever "forget the moment when the vehicles rolled out of camp, with the parents trying in one last gaze to fix an image to last for eternity."[41]

Then French officials made a new demand that the French would only offer exit visas for Jewish children who were bona fide orphans and had their parent's death certificates to prove it.[42] Fifty suitable candidates were found.

The Quakers hired the *Serpa Pinto*, a Portuguese ship of 8,200 tons with a length of 467 feet, to transport the 50 Jewish orphans from Lisbon to the U.S. The Quakers contracted me to act as the children's physician on this fateful ocean crossing.

Unfortunately, after American troops invaded North Africa on November 8, 1942, the French Vichy government cut off diplomatic relations with the United States and then denied the Jewish children their French exit visas. The Quakers waited several months for the Jewish children, but it became clear that the French would not allow the children to leave France. On my 41st birthday, January 17, 1943, the *Serpa Pinto* set sail for America with only a few passengers and a cargo of cork. The Quaker personnel and the few refugees traveling along were distraught and deeply saddened that they could not save these 50 innocent children. Subsequently many of these children were undoubtedly among the one million Jewish children murdered by the Nazis.

37 Lowrie, *The Hunted Children*, 208

38 Samuel, *Rescuing the Children: A Holocaust Memoir*, Kindle location 1685

39 Suback, *Relief and Rescue*, Kindle location 1996.

40 Dr. Joseph Weill's account is in Samuel, *Rescuing the Children: A Holocaust Memoir*." Kindle location 1824

41 Lowrie, *The Hunted Children*, 217. Rev. Henri Manen, a Protestant pastor in Aix-en-Provence testified that on August 10, 1942, he saw "'a tall, good-looking boy of seventeen or eighteen standing between his father and mother, with his arm around her neck. He is not crying. But he bends over the one then over the other, rubbing his face against theirs, slowly and gently, with all the tenderness in the world. Not a word. The father and mother continue to weep silently....Finally the bus rumbles off.' Manen noted the remark of an ashen-faced policeman: 'I have seen massacres, the war, [and] famine. I have never seen anything as horrible as that.'" Adam Rayski, *The Choice of the Jews Under Vichy: Between Submission and Resistance*, (University of Notre Dame Press, 2015), 109.

42 Jews that were killed in German concentration camps did not receive death certificates.

Sailing to America: January 1943

After a few days at sea, our ship, the *Serpa Pinto*, was stopped by a German U-boat in international waters, and several German officers boarded, sending the Jewish refugees on the ship into a state of panic. The Germans spoke to the captain and then they all retired to the captain's cabin. We learned later that the Germans inspected the passenger list, but to our relief they took no action and left. We remained in a state of paranoid fear for the remainder of the voyage.

This boarding by the Germans took place in January 1943, at the height of the Battle of the Atlantic. Virtually all Allied merchant ships crossed the Atlantic by convoy to avoid German submarines. The *Serpa Pinto* was a neutral vessel and was not torpedoed by German U-boats because it flew a clearly visible Portuguese flag that was well illuminated at night.

Two weeks later, we arrived safely in America. We were not welcomed by the Statue of Liberty, as newcomers usually are. The Port of New York was closed, so instead we came up the Delaware River to Philadelphia. We were too anxious to kneel down and kiss the soil of the Promised Land. We were very worried about finding suitable housing, managing the language barrier, and finding a job. Not to mention that we had no money whatsoever.

American immigration officials boarded the *Serpa Pinto* and began their usual formalities of clearing the passenger list. The travelers were called one by one, and all the passengers left the ship that first day except for us. The officials informed us that there was an administrative delay requiring that we sleep aboard the ship for another night.

The following day there was no change. I was troubled and spoke to the ship's captain. He did not know what was causing our delay, and he encouraged me to speak directly with the American immigration officials.

I could not speak English, so a French Naval officer who was in the vicinity acted as an interpreter. We informed them that Gisy had siblings living in Chicago. Unbeknownst to us, our delay was caused by my open FBI investigation, and the FBI quickly dispatched an agent to visit Gisy's relatives in Chicago. When the FBI agent arrived, he interrogated Emil's wife, Greta. She misconstrued the nature of the questioning and was afraid that she was the one under investigation and at risk of being sent back to Vienna. The FBI agent explained to Greta that they were investigating me, and not her, and that I was being held at a ship docked in Philadelphia. Greta told the agent that I was her brother-in-law.

Two days later, the agent questioned Gisy's brother Frank after he returned from work. Frank admitted that he had contacted Elmer Karp, asking him to falsely swear that he was related to me. After receiving Frank's statement, the FBI agent closed the investigation.

A U.S. immigration official in Philadelphia had a copy of that blue document which had also been in our application file at the U.S. Consulate in Marseilles. The letter said that Dr. Karp was under investigation by the FBI, and that until the matter was resolved, no entry to the United States could be allowed. Therefore, the immigration officer denied my entry until a relative vouched that I was not a spy.

Three days after we arrived in Philadelphia, a group of American immigration officials and a customs officer met with us. They inspected our papers and allowed us to disembark. The customs officer confiscated a bottle of port, which was a gift from our friends in Lisbon. This was an illegal action, as it was perfectly legal to import one bottle of liquor per person. We took this loss with grace and hoped that the gentlemen enjoyed our wine.

As we exited the ship, we met a local Philadelphia cop who spoke to us in Yiddish. I had never met or even heard of a Jewish policeman in France, Austria, Hungary, or Romania. It was frankly inconceivable to me, and I was overjoyed and filled with confidence that we would be accepted in our new country.

The weather in Philadelphia was snowy and cold and we were not prepared with the appropriate clothing. The Jewish policeman helped us buy a warm sweater for Susie.

We received an official American stamp of entry on January 29, 1943. Free at last. We were now safe in our new country.

Opposite page: *My travel documents including a US visa, A Spanish stamp on November 22, 1942 at Aduana de Valencia de Alcantara, a transit visa for Portugal, and proof of admission to the United States in Philadelphia on January 29, 1943.*

Immigration Visa
ection XXXXXXXXX XXXX
6(a) (3)
manian N° -47-
quota
ated OCT 2 1942

ssued to Adolf KARP
(name)

Leonard G. Bradford
American Vice Consul
Marseille, France

ESTA PROHIBIDA EN ESPAÑA
LA IMPORTACION Y EXPORTACION
DE BILLETES DE BANCO ESPAÑOLES Y PLATA

1060
a favor de A. Karp
o en este Consulado de España Bueno
Portugal en tránsito
España, sin facultad de detenerse,
ando por la frontera de Canfranc
diendo por Caldas
rizado en

arsella a 10 de Noviembre 194.2
El Consul de España,

V. VIA VENTALLO

CONSULADO DE ESPAÑA
MARSELLA

DERECHOS CONS
MARSELLA
del Aransel

Ar.
Dispos   A.22
Cambio aplicado e
Francos 84

DUANA de VALENCIA de ALCANTARA

EL TITULAR DE ESTE PASAPORTE SALE
ESPAÑA SIN DIVISAS
A DE 22 NOV. 1942

Pasageiro em Transito

P.V.D.E.-SECÇÃO INTERNACIONAL
MARVÃO-BEIRA

VISTO BOM para Portugal, em transito p
New-York autorisaçao telegraf.
da P.V.D.E. No. 33490 de 5 de XI de 19
VALIDO por 30 dias, Consulado de Portu
em Marselha 7 de Novembro de 1942

CONSULADO DA REPUBLICA PORTUGUESA
MARSELHA

Pagou ao cambio de Frs 1,60... Frs 120
Art. 12 a 82 N° da receita. 3088 9
Art. N° 117 9
Art. N° 115 280
Total Frs 409

CONSULADO
7 NOV 5$00
SERVICO CONSULAR
MARSELHA

PUESTO DE POLICIA DE VALENCIA DE ALCÁNTARA
Zona Sur S.P.F.P.A.
2 NOV. 1942
SALIDA EN TRANSITO
NUM. 3902 VISE:

S/S Serpa Pinto
Admitted at Philadel Pa.
on JAN 29 1943 upon presenta
of Sec 6 quota immIGRATION VISA
No. 47
Frederick E. Disbr
Immigrant Ineli

P.V.D.E.
SERVIÇO DE ESTRANGEIROS
SENHA N. LU. 125
Visto em Transito
Valido por 15 dias
Lisboa 23/1/42
O ADJUNTO

P.V.D.E.
SERVIÇO DE ESTRANGEIROS
SENHA N. M.C. 36
Visto em Transito
Valido por 15 dias
Lisboa 9/12/42
O ADJUNTO

P.V.D.E.
SERVIÇO DE ESTRANGEIROS
SENHA N. M.G. 12
Visto em Transito
Valido por 15 dias
Lisboa 26/12/42
O ADJUNTO

REPUBLICA PORTUGUESA

Visto N°
via
Governo Civil de Lisboa JAN 1943
SECRETARI
Selos 50$00
Emol 40$00
ind

Bundesarchiv, Bild 101I-027-1477-04 | Foto: Vennemann, Wolfgang | January 1943

Roundup of Jews in the Vieux Port *who were then loaded onto cattle cars at the Marseille train station. All photographs in this chapter are courtesy of the Bundesarchiv Koblenz. All are dated January and February, 1943. The Germans kept copious written records and photographs of their activities.*

Bundesarchiv, Bild 101I-027-1473-05 | Foto: Vennemann, Wolfgang | January 1943

Battle of Marseille:
January 23, 1943

NEW CHAPTER FOR REVISED EDITION WRITTEN BY LARRY BERNSTEIN

I n mid-January 1943 during the *Serpa Pinto's* ocean crossing, *SS-Sturmbannführer* Bernhard Griese met with Marseille's acting prefect for municipal affairs, Pierre Barraud, and the secretary general of the French police, René Bousquet. Together they planned the arrest of the Jewish population in Marseille.

Bundesarchiv, Bild 1011-027-1477-07 | Foto: Ven neman, Wolfgang | 24 January 1943

On January 23, 1943, nearly two thousand Jews were arrested in Marseille in an operation called Action Tiger. The Jews were identified by the red Jewish stamp on their French identity cards and then they were detained.

Here is how Raymond-Raoul Lambert described what happened in Marseille in his diary: "On Saturday, January 23, [1943], buses moving through the streets after curfew caused people to suspect that unusual operations were being organized. In the morning we were told there had been police raids in many downtown neighborhoods. All Jews, French or foreign, were systematically arrested. This police operation had been prepared meticulously and with the utmost rigor by the authorities. Locksmiths were requisitioned to open the doors of houses whose occupants were presumed to be pretending to be away. These operations were in full swing between 11 pm and 5 am. Women were taken away in the police vans without having had time to dress; the sick were forced out of their beds; old people were taken away forcibly, and parents were separated from their children."[43]

The Jews were then escorted by the French police to a Marseille train station. Cattle cars were waiting for them there, which were then filled to capacity. The cattle cars had no seats, no water, and no toilets, so passengers had to relieve themselves on the floor.[44] The trains headed first to a French-run detention camp in northern France before the Jews were sent to their deaths in the German concentration camps.[45]

After the Jews were removed from Marseille, the Germans failed to maintain order with the remaining residents in the *Vieux Port*. The local Algerians, who had little loyalty to the French, should have been easy allies, but the Germans inflicted the same harsh treatment on them that they used elsewhere. When the Germans patrolled the *Vieux Port* in regular intervals, the locals learned their patterns, attacked them, and then disappeared in the maze. Stronger German patrols were sent but to no avail, as the underground passages were so intricate that only the natives knew where they led.

The Germans did not find a solution for this harassment. In February 1943, the Germans blew up the *Vieux Port* with the aid of the French police. After the war, the port was rebuilt but the new structure does not replicate the original port's old world charm.

René Bousquet, the head of the French Police during the Battle of Marseille, was arrested and tried immediately after the war for collaborating with the Germans. He was sentenced to prison for five years but was almost immediately granted amnesty. Years later, Bousquet became active in French left wing politics, and was a close personal confidant of French President François Mitterrand. In 1993, the French government charged Bousquet with crimes against humanity, but just before his trial started, he was assassinated.

The German massacre of the Jewish population of France depended on the collaboration of the French local police, its civil service and its civilian leadership.[46] In her book *The Holocaust, the French and the Jews*, Susan Zuccotti estimates that 24% of France's 330,000 prewar population of French Jewish citizens perished in the Holocaust. Among the 135,000 foreign Jewish refugees in France, she estimates 41-45% were killed.[47]

The Jews killed in France included mothers and fathers, children, and grandparents. Some were French war veterans who had served in the various French wars with distinction.[48]

The historian Donna Ryan in her book, *The Holocaust & the Jews of Marseille*, concludes "the implementation of Hitler's 'Final Solution to the Jewish Question' succeeded...*because of*, not in spite of, French initiatives. By despising, labeling, segregating, and incarcerating Jews, French officials took a path of bigotry that led many of their victims to the death camps. Auschwitz was not the only possible terminus for that route, but the death camps couldn't have existed without the first steps of segregation and expulsion....On a balance sheet of blame for the implementation of the Final Solution in southern France, Vichy authorities would have to accept much guilt. The French government and its law enforcement branches took slow but deliberate steps that consistently aided the Germans. Few actions by officials in Marseille hampered the Nazis or helped Jews....French officials did not intend the final step— genocide—but they deliberately participated in the phases leading up to it....In their zeal to reduce Jewish influence, seize Jewish assets, and drive all foreign elements from the country and in their eagerness to get the best possible deal for France in the New Europe, they prepared all the groundwork for the Nazis and the Holocaust."[49]

Bild 101I-027-1477-16 | Photographer: Vennemann, Wolfgang | 24. Januar 1943

Opposite page:
This list of deportees from Marseille
includes people born from Salonica,
Constantinople, Oran, Algiers, and
various French cities. Courtesy of
Serge Klarsfeld, Memorial to the
Jews Deported from France,
1942–1944, p. 414.

43 Raymond-Raoul Lambert was the director of the Jewish Agency, the Union générale des israélites de France, which was located in Marseille. His diary was published posthumously with the title *Book a Witness: 1940-1943*, (Ivan R. Dee 2007), 164. Raymond Raoul Lambert and his family were subsequently deported and murdered in Auschwitz after they were sent in convoy number 64 from the French camp at Drancy on December 7, 1943. Raymond Raoul Lambert was the same man who signed the letter that confirmed that Dr. Karp worked for the Jewish Agency's Marseille medical clinic that can be seen in the exhibit on p. 83.

44 Kitson, *Police and Politics in Marseille 1936-1945*, 154 and Donna P. Ryan in *The Holocaust and the Jews of Marseille*, University of Illinois Press, 1996, 4.

45 Survival rates from Convoys 52 and 53 from Drancy to German concentration camps were typical. Convoy 52 left with 997 Jews of which 780 were from Marseille and 570 were French citizens. Convoy 53 included 999 Jews of which 580 were French citizens and 119 were children. By 1945, there were no survivors from Convoy 52 and five survivors from Convoy 53. Three of the five survivors had escaped from the train. Edith Thomas wrote in a contemporaneous letter that "I saw a train pass [and in the] front, a car containing French police and German soldiers. Then came cattle cars, sealed. The thin arms of children clasped the grating. A hand waved outside like a leaf in a storm. When the train slowed down, voices cried 'Mama!' And nothing answered except the squeaking of the springs....The truth: stars worn on breasts, children torn from their mothers, men shot every day, the methodical degradation of an entire people. The truth is censored. We must cry it from the rooftops." Paxton, *Vichy France: Old Guard and New Order, 1940-1944*, Kindle location 3315 or p. 183.

Martin Gilbert wrote that "the Germans had mocked Marseille as the 'new Jerusalem of the Mediterranean,' where the Jews 'reigned as lords of the cafes and restaurants, waiting for the victory of the Americans.' Now these Jews, many of them refugee children, were held in detention camps, awaiting deportation....At La Rose, four miles east of Marseille, thirty Jewish orphans were seized, together with their guardian Alice Salomon, who insisted on sharing their fate." Martin Gilbert, *The Holocaust, A History of the Jews of Europe During the Second World War* (Henry Holt & Co., 1986), 530.

46 The preparations for mass murder were made possible by Germany's military successes following the invasion of Poland in 1939. But from the moment that Adolf Hitler had come to power in Germany in 1933, the devastating process had begun. It was a process which depended upon the rousing of historic hatreds and ancient prejudice, and upon the cooperation or acquiescence of many different forces: of industry, science and medicine, of the Civil Service and bureaucracy, and of the modern mechanisms and channels of communication. It depended also upon collaborators from countries far beyond the German border; and it depended most of all, one survivor has remarked, 'upon the indifference of bystanders in every land.'" Gilbert, *The Holocaust*, 18.

47 8,000 to 10,000 Jewish children were saved thanks to Jewish organizations that helped them emigrate overseas, to cross into Switzerland or Spain, or were "entrusted through the intervention of clandestine networks to non-Jewish families or institutions (convents, secular institutions)." Samuel, *Rescuing the Children: A Holocaust Memoir*, Kindle location 2764 or p. 132

48 Luckily most of the doctors at the Marseille clinic escaped deportation. In *Rescue and Flight* (Kindle location 2050), Susan Subak quotes René Zimmer's report that "the physicians and surgeons Wolff, Mendel and Landmann had gone into hiding or joined the [Maquis]. Dr. [George] Karp had made it to Lisbon and Dr. Baer to Switzerland....with the terrible exception of our medical secretary Madame Haber, who was deported along with her husband." See also René Zemmer's report of current activities to the Unitarian Service that is available online at the Harvard University Library http://pds.lib. harvard.edu/pds/view/25341753?n=10&printThumbnails=no.

49 Ryan, *The Holocaust and The Jews of Marseille*, xi and 220.

List of Deportees, Convoy 52

NOM DE FAMILLE	PREMIER NOM	DATE DE NAISSANCE	LIEU DE NAISSANCE	CITOYENNETTE
ABASTADO	DINA	21.08.16	SALONIQUE	G
ABASTADO	JACQUES	17.06.07	SALONIQUE	F
ABECASSIS	JACQUES	16.04.23	PARIS	F
ABECASSIS	ISAAC	12.02.21	ORAN	F
ABIGNOLI	FORTUNEE	03.01.90	LE CAIRE	F
ABIMELEK	ELICZER	18.07.92	BROUSSE	F
ABIMELEK	MAURICE	30.08.24	MARSEILLE	F.
ABISSEROR	ROSALIE	15.11.10	ORAN	F
ABOUAF	RACHEL	18.04.90	CONSTANTINOPLE	F
ABOUAV	MICHON	24.05.05	CONSTANTINOPLE	T
ABOUAV	MAURICE	13.05.27	LYON	T
ABOUAV	RACHEL	24.05.25	LYON	T
ABOUAV	ZELDA	15.10.28	EPINAY/S	F
ABRAMOVITCH	BERNARD	09.02.74	KHODEL	P
ABRANOWICZ	MARIA	.75	ODESSA	P
ACHACH	JOSEPH	01.07.07	ORAN	F
ACHACHE	ALBERT	07.01.24	OUJDA	F
ACHACHE	ANDRE	04.10.21	OUJDA	F
ACHACHE	FANNY	07.04.23	ORAN	F
ACHACHE	SIMHA	.81	TLEMCEN	F
ACHOUR	HERMANCE	09.04.12	ORAN	F
ACHOUR	JACOB	26.01.03	ORAN	F
ACHOUR	RAOUL	26.10.10	MARSEILLE	F
ADEVAK	ABRAHAM	27.04.10	CONSTANTIN	F
ADJEB	MELLIA	.01	ALGER	F
ADLER	MAURICE	01.12.82	KOZENIEZ	T
ADOUT	CHAOUL	.03.09	FLOVDIC	BU
ADOUT	MARDOU	.05.81	FLOVDIC	BU
AELION	ESTERINE		SALONIQUE	G
AFRIAT	MOISE	06.12.11	ORAN	F
AGAI	FANNY	09.11.86	ST LOUIS	F
AGAI	JOSEPH	18.09.82	ORAN	F
AKNIN	FELIX	15.04.84	ALGER	F
AKNIN	DAEMRA	05.06.88	TLEMCEN	F
AKNINE	DAVID	06.03.00	TLEMCEN	F
AKNINE	MESSAOUD	06.10.70	TANGER	F
AKOKA	GILBERT	10.03.22	MARSEILLE	F
AKOKA	JULIE	31.01.90	ALGER	F
AKOUN	HELENE	23.01.18	ORAN	F
ALBOU	ALBERT	28.02.21	MARSEILLE	F
ALBOU	ARMAND	12.11.23	MARSEILLE	F
ALBOU	FREHA	31.12.78	SIDI-BEL-ABBES	F
ALBOU	LEON	27.04.14	MARSEILLE	F
ALBOU	MAURICE	09.11.10	MARSEILLE	F
ALBOUY	SIMON	19.11.02	ALGER	F
ALLOUCHE	MORCHI	01.12.00	AINBUDA	F
ALMOSNINO	MORDOHAI	15.09.10	SALONIQUE	F
ALMOSNINO	SOL	31.12.83	SALONIQUE	G
ALVO	SENTOV	17.05.98	SALONIQUE	G
AMADIA	HENRIETTE	02.03.90	SOUSSE	F
AMAR	DAVID	21.09.10	MARSEILLE	F
AMAR	SAMUEL	26.03.12	ORAN	F
AMOYAL	ABRAHAM	03.03.08	SIDI-BEL-ABBES	F
AMSALLEM	ISIDORE	25.06.05	ORAN	F
AMSEL	RACHEL	15.02.82	VARSOVIE	P
AMSELLEM	JACOB	09.06.86	MEDA	F
ANDERMAN	BRONIA	13.09.06	BUEZAZ	P
ANUDAY	GASTON	04.08.06	AIN-SEFRA	F
ARAMA	ABRAHAM	02.02.13	SALONIQUE	F
ARAMA	DOUDOUN	.89	SALONIQUE	F
ARAMA	ISAAC	10.12.15	SALONIQUE	F
ARAMA	SNOCHAN	.81	SALONIQUE	G
ARAMA	SYLVIA	.12.12	SALONIQUE	F
ARANOWICZ	MAJER	29.08.96	LARIK	P
ARBITI	JOSEPH	08.09.13	ALEP	F
AROCHAS	DJOYA	12.12.93	SMYRNE	F
AROCHAS	ELVIRE	09.09.25	MARSEILLE	F
AROCHAS	HAIM	.87	SMYRNE	F
ARON	MADELEINE	11.08.91	PARIS	F
AROVAS	NISSIM	10.10.06	CONSTANTINOPLE	F
ARROVAS	CLARA	20.02.01	CONSTANTINOPLE	F
ARROVAS	GEORGES	11.07.25	MARSEILLE	F
ARROVAS	JACQUES	28.01.95	CONSTANTINOPLE	F
ARROVAS	VICTORIA	18.01.22	CONSTANTINOPLE	F
ASSA	ESTHER	.05.89	CONSTANTINOPLE	F
ASSA	JACQUES	28.08.22	LIMA	F
ASSA	LAZARE	16.03.21	LIMA	F
ASSA	LEON	18.10.80	CONSTANTINOPLE	F
ASSA	ROBERT	25.08.13	MARSEILLE	F
ASSARAF	DJOAR	10.01.87	ORAN	F
ATHIAS	JACQUES	12.03.22	SETEF	F
ATOUM	ELIE	.99	ISTAMBOUL	F
ATTIAS	RENNE	06.06.28	MARSEILLE	F
ATTIAS	CAMERA	.95	OURMEL	F
AUSTER LERNER	MENDEL	31.01.79	ZALUKIEW	P
AYACHE	MESSAOUDA	03.01.81	ORAN	F
AZAN	MARIE	17.12.05	ST DENIS	F
AZAR	AVRAM	15.08.08	TIRI	F
AZIZA	EMILE	17.03.06	ORAN	F
AZIZA	JOSEPHINE	24.01.10	ST LUCIEN	F
AZOULAI	AARON	28.08.79	ORAN	F
AZOULAY	CHARLES	19.01.09	MARSEILLE	F
AZOULAY	DAVID	.94	TAFIBALIT	F
AZOULAY	ESTHER	21.06.90	MARSEILLE	F
AZOULAY	HENRI	14.10.77	ALGER	F
AZOULAY	PAULETTE	01.05.19	MARSEILLE	F
AZOUZ	DOUDOU	.79	SALONIQUE	G
AZOUZ	SIMON	18.03.77	THESSALONIKI	G
AZUELOS	MOISE	15.03.09	ORAN	F
AZULAI	ISRAEL	23.06.92	MEDECI	F
BACRI	ABRAHAM	09.01.93	ALGER	F
BACRI	ELEONORE	16.02.94	ALGER	F
BACRI	MEYER	21.06.80	BLIDA	F
BACRI	WILLIAM	01.01.23	ALGER	F
BAJGELMAN	LESER	.95	RYHI	P
BALTER	JOSEPH	27.08.96	LECRUAY	P
BAND	BERTHA	23.04.75	LINZ	AUT
BARBER	FISCHEL	01.05.99	JDUMSKA	F
BARCHAY	ESTHER	.78	KIEW	R
BARCHAY	LEIB	.75	BARISSOF	R
BARMET	ABRAHAM	07.09.79	RUSSIE	A
BARMET	REFKA	19.09.79	SKALAT	P
BAROUH	ELDA	15.07.11	SALONIQUE	T
BAROUH	SALOMON	09.11.05	CONSTANTINOPLE	T
BARUCHEL	JULIE	12.12.98	ORAN	F
BARUCHEL	YOUMTOBE	27.04.76	ALGER	F
BARZILAI	MAURICE	10.12.21	SALONIQUE	G
BARZILAI	DOUDOU	21.03.09	SALONIQUE	G
BARZILAY	LIESER	.11	SALONIQUE	G
BARZILAY	MIRIAM	02.10.19	SALONIQUE	G
BAUMGARTL	THERESE	19.01.81	IGLAU	AUT
BAUMGARTZ	CHARLES	03.07.76	BENESCHAU	AUT
BAUSTEIN	SIEGFRIED	23.03.14	VIENNE	AUT
BEGA	JUDA	15.04.09	FERRIA	F
BEHAR	ALBERT	06.05.23	SALONIQUE	G
BEHAR	DAVID	24.08.22	MARSEILLE	F
BEHAR	GILDA	11.10.25	MARSEILLE	F
BEHAR	MARCELLE	25.11.16	MARSEILLE	F
BEHAR	SALOMON	03.08.90	SALONIQUE	G
BEJA	MAURICE	03.02.21	SALONIQUE	G
BEL AISZ	DAVID	11.02.88	BONE	F
BEL AISZ	ROLAND	12.07.25	BONE	F
BENAHAIM	ALBERT	12.02.82	TANGER	F
BENAICH	FERNAND	03.06.10	MARSEILLE	F
BENAICH	JOSEPH	13.10.12	AVIGNON	F
BEN-AICH	MAURICE	27.01.06	MARSEILLE	F
BENAICH	SARA	15.05.08	TETOUAN	F
BENAICH	SARAH	01.01.22	CUBA	F
BEZARDOUTH	LEA	23.01.03	SALONIQUE	G
BEN ASAYAL	DAVID	14.05.01	ALGER	F
BENASRA	ALBERT	10.04.09	MASCARA	F
BENASRA	ANDRE	19.12.15	MASCARA	F
BENASRA	LUCIEN	12.12.25	MASCARA	F
BENAYOUM	ALBERT	04.04.08	FRENDA	F
BENAYOUM	JOSEPH	30.08.86	ORAN	F
BENDAHAN	ALBERT	03.11.11	DRAN	F
BENDAHAN	JACOB	17.05.97	BOU-SAADA	F
BEN DAHAN	MESSAOUDA	03.09.71	ALGER	F
BEN DAVID	EMILE	24.12.10	NICE	F
BENDAVID	LOUISE	15.11.08	MARSEILLE	F
BENDAVID	VIDAL	17.02.07	MARSEILLE	F
BENDAYAN	EMILE	18.10.02	ORAN	F
BENEZRA	BEHOR	30.11.04	TURQUIE	F
BENEZRA	MARIE	03.04.26	MARSEILLE	F
BENFORADO	JOSEPH	.73	SALONIQUE	G
BENFORADO	MARGUERITE	15.09.15	SALONIQUE	G
BENGAS	MOISE	.04	VERRIA	F
BENGUIGUI	AARON	08.02.87	ORAN	F
BENGUIGUI	ALBERT	05.01.02	ORAN	F
BENGUIGUI	ELIE	10.02.21	ORAN	F
BENGUIGUI	MOUCHI	15.06.15	TLEMCEN	F
BENHAIM	CHARLES	13.10.21	ORAN	F
BENHAIM	DAVID	14.05.11	ORAN	F
BENHAIM	ESTHER	11.02.24	ORAN	F
BEN-HAIM	GASTON	31.07.02	St EUGENE	F
BENHAIM	GEORGES	10.09.16	MARSEILLE	F
BENHAIM	JULIE	22.10.92	ORAN	F
BENHAIM	MAURICE	27.04.26	MARSEILLE	F
BENHAMOU	DAVID	26.07.88	MOSTAGANEM	F
BENHAMOU	LEON	21.07.96	MARINA	F
BENHAMOU	LEONIE	06.01.81	TLEMCEN	F
BENHAMOU	NATHAN	28.01.10	MARNIA	F
BENICHOU	ADOLPHE	14.12.21	PARIS	F

A New Life in America: Post 1943

My parents named me Adolf. But after the rise of Adolf Hitler, I became increasingly disgusted by own first name. Upon arriving in America, one of my first official acts was to change my name from Adolf to George. I figured that George must be an acceptable first name as it is shared by America's first president, George Washington.

The Philadelphia Jewish Relief Agency found us accommodations and gave us some money. There was much to do. We needed to learn English, and American culture, and make the necessary arrangements so I could practice medicine. Gisy had a good working knowledge of English from her school days, but did not think she was fluent enough to speak in public. Our lodgings had a kitchen, and Gisy prepared the meals while I bought the groceries. Gisy was amazed at my shopping success even though I did not know any English, but she quickly discovered that I could converse in my rusty Yiddish with the local Jewish grocery store owner.

Frank Tiger.   *Emil Tiger.*

In the meantime, I set to work learning English. I spoke to everyone who would listen, went to the movies to hear the cadence of spoken English, and read the newspapers. In short, I used the same process to learn English as I had done with French.

A Viennese couple heard of our arrival in Philadelphia and wanted to meet us. One day our bell rang, and these complete strangers greeted us with a large grocery bag filled with baked goods. This was a very warm welcome in a strange country, which made us feel more confident that we had a future here. Some old friends from Vienna also lived in town, and we enjoyed dinners with them, and a lovely evening at the Philadelphia Symphony Orchestra.[50] It was incredible that only a few weeks before we were being hunted by the Nazis, and now we were enjoying delicious food, spending time with friends, and exploring our new city.

I met with the Quakers to review our failure to secure the 50 Jewish children in Lisbon. Like us, they were greatly disappointed. The Quakers asked me to speak to their high schools about our escape, which I did with pleasure.

Gisy's sister, Sophie, offered to move her family from La Crosse, Wisconsin, to Chicago

The Tiger siblings and their spouses. From top left: Bill Falber (Sophie's husband), George, Gisy, Max, Greta (Emil's wife), Emil, Frank, Clara, Sophie Falber, Beatrice (Max's wife) and Inga (Frank's wife).

if we agreed to move to Chicago as well. Gisy was very close to Sophie, so our decision was easy. We looked forward to a homecoming in Chicago. Two of Gisy's brothers, Frank and Emil, and their wives, Inga and Greta, were already living in town. Sophie, her husband, Bill, and her daughter, Dita, moved into the same apartment building that we lived in.

Emil and Frank were quickly drafted into the U.S. army. They were given the choice to go to the Atlantic or the Pacific theater. The army asked Emil if he would do undercover intelligence work in Europe because of his strong language skills and local knowledge. Both brothers had spent years trying to get away from Hitler's Europe, and were very concerned about their fate if they were captured alive by the Germans, so they both shipped out on the same boat to fight the Japanese.

It was necessary for me to take a medical license exam. The Illinois test was a written exam unlike the verbal test in Vienna. Many of the European doctors who took the exam failed repeatedly because they did not study properly, but I passed after my first try because I properly prepared.

Unfortunately, it was also necessary that I repeat my medical internship. This delayed the opening of my private practice by an additional year. The income from my internship was insufficient to cover my family's ongoing expenses. This requirement was frustrating and completely unnecessary as I had already completed a one-year internship, five years of rotating residency, and practiced medicine in Vienna and France for several years. Gisy found a job working at the B'nai B'rith in Chicago. It was important to her to support Jewish charities, particularly because they had been so critical to our escape from Europe.

I received an internship at Columbus Hospital in Chicago, and I was initially assigned to the obstetrical department's night service. When a pregnant patient arrived at the hospital, an intern on duty would do an examination and then notify the attending physician. On one particular late night, the attending physician gave me instructions which I did not understand because of my poor English. I asked the attending nurse for help in the matter, but she was unwilling or unable to explain. So, I called my closest friend and woke him up to ask for help. He burst into hysterics when he found out the unknown procedure was an enema. I was baffled afterwards why the nurse was unhelpful and did not use sign language.

It took months to find out the results of my medical exams, so I worked part-time jobs. I did physicals for new workers at the American Transportation Corporation, and was employed by the health department for the Chicago Public Schools. In those days, when a child contracted a contagious disease, they were quarantined. A sign was put on the front stoop warning people not to enter the residence. I went to the homes of the children with chicken pox, measles, mumps, and scarlet fever to determine if the children were healthy enough to return to school. At this time, there were no vaccines and these diseases were extremely dangerous and potentially fatal. The freedom to find your choice of employment here in America was incredible to me. This really was the Promised Land.

Shortly after I received my medical license, I opened an office on Western Avenue. Nobody knew me; I had no friends, patients, or other connections to refer new patients to me. Accordingly my reception room was empty. It was a lonely, dispiriting time, and only on rare occasions did a patient walk in from the street.

Soon after, I moved my medical office to the second floor of an apartment building on Devon Avenue. It was a converted apartment, up a narrow stairway that had a reception room that I shared with a dentist. Many physicians had been drafted into the armed forces, creating a doctor shortage. As a result, my office to my surprise soon became very busy. I worked six days a week. Mornings I spent in the hospital and afternoons in the office. Evening hours were routine, and after a short interval for dinner, I worked late, on occasion until midnight. At that time, I delivered babies, did minor surgery, and of course, went on house calls. For several families, I took care of the children that I delivered.

As a doctor you have to keep your eyes open for trouble. One elderly female patient of mine was being prepared for surgery to heal her hemorrhoids. Early on the morning of the surgery, I entered her room and noticed that her left eyebrow was shaved. She shared a room with another older woman who was also heading into surgery. I asked this women about her surgical preparation, and she informed me that she was in the hospital for a cataract procedure. She was completely baffled as to why a nurse had asked her to turn over and then shaved her anus. Clearly, the surgical procedures for the two women had been mixed up. I promptly resolved the matter, but I lost my patient. She never sought my medical advice again.

I was happy to work hard and anxious to save money. In due time, my medical practice provided a secure and comfortable life for our family. By 1948, we had saved

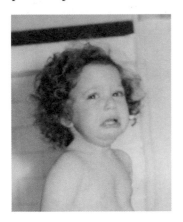

enough money to buy a home. A year later, we were properly settled and decided to have more children. Our two beautiful daughters, Erica and Sharon, were born thirteen months apart between 1949 and 1950.

Gisy went into labor at home on August 11,1950. It was late afternoon, and Erica had just woken from her nap. She saw her mother was about to leave the house, so she began throwing a fit. She started screaming and crying. But, we had to leave for the hospital, so we walked out the door. Erica stood by the window having an enormous tantrum, screaming and pounding on the glass, her red curls flying. Susie tried to comfort her to no avail. The neighbors probably thought Susie was torturing her!

The car pulled away, Gisy waved goodbye. As we entered the parking lot, she said, "The baby is coming now!" The obstetrician, a very close friend, Dr. Pessel, was on his way to the hospital to deliver the baby, but hadn't yet arrived. The ER people ran out with a stretcher, and helped Gisy on it. I then delivered my own baby girl, my beautiful Sharon, right there in the parking lot of Frank Cuneo Hospital!

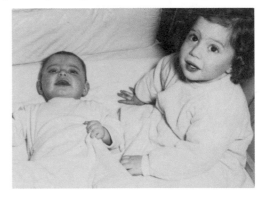

In America, we made new friends, traveled, and enjoyed our family. Our life here has been a very good one. Like many immigrants who arrived in the United States with nothing, I worked, saved, and invested so I could retire comfortably.

Over four decades, I developed a successful family medical practice. Curing a patient was extremely gratifying, but the death of a patient, whether expected or unexpected, was always a personal blow, and I deeply felt the family's sorrow. I received appreciation from my patients, but was not fully aware of how much they cared for me until I announced my retirement at the age of 80. Then there was such an outpouring of love, as well as sincere regret, that I felt deep satisfaction for my efforts, far more than ever before.

It is more difficult to assess my patients in psychoanalysis. Many of my patients are grateful because they are successfully managing their careers, raising their children, and improving their marriages. Those who are not doing as well do not stay in touch with me. Psychoanalysis does not show easily measured results, and sometimes none at all. However, the individual's condition may improve over time even long after treatment is completed.

It is a pity that currently the teachings of Sigmund Freud are so heavily criticized, often based on ignorance or ill will. Freud's profound influence on modern psychology is frequently ignored or misinterpreted, and I expect Freudian theory and practices will eventually make a comeback.

I am encouraged by the increasing popularity of a more inclusive approach to treating patients, coined "Holistic Medicine," thus reviving this oldest type of medical practice. As both a general physician and as a psychoanalyst, I combined the treatment of mind and body in my practice. I believe a doctor needs to understand the full picture of mental and physical health to determine the proper diagnosis and appropriate treatment.

One critical role of a great physician is to provide hope to the sick. To combine truth and hope in the practice of medicine is an art. The physician must treat each patient as an individual first and foremost; the disease, pain, and suffering are secondary. Excellent training and professional medical knowledge alone are insufficient.

---

50 These old friends were Fritz and Trude Baumohl who had also escaped from Marseille. Fritz is the one who informed us of the Algerian forger in the *Vieux Port* who manufactured our counterfeit French exit visas.

Conclusion

Without question, family life has been my most rewarding experience. Gisy and I have loved every moment spent with our three daughters. I revel in my grandchildren. I hope they succeed beyond their wildest dreams.

Looking back now, I see my successes, my disappointments, and my regrets. My aim was always to give love and attention to the people around me. I received an abundance of love from my mother, my wife, and my children. I depend on love for sustenance and joy, so perhaps I have an exaggerated notion of love's importance in life. But I suspect many people have similar sentiments, and that we all need to feel loved.

It has been a pleasure to write my life story. I hope my children and grandchildren will read this book, and when they do, my efforts will have been worthwhile. Gisy and I were lucky to have many relatives survive the war. Gisy's parents and all of her siblings managed to escape. A couple of my cousins immigrated to Palestine, but most of our cousins, distant relatives, as well as most of our Jewish friends and acquaintances were murdered by the Germans.

Susie's wedding photo: (from left to right) Erica, Susie, Gisy, Sharon and me.

Although I survived, I was scarred. I had my first nightmare in Puigcerdà, the night I realized that my simple escape plan to Spain was not going to work. Since then I have had recurring nightmares. In my dreams, I find that my life as a doctor in Chicago was only a temporary reprieve, and that at any moment, I would be dragged back to a concentration camp. My paranoid fear of persecution continues to this day.

In my youth I had many happy times in Sibiu, and prior to the rise of the Nazis, I had a very serene life in Vienna. I was stunned when the Nazis successfully tapped into the Austrian and German latent anti-Semitism, unleashing incredible violence.

My last few years in Europe were an unrelenting nightmare, as we were so frightened and desperate to escape from the Nazi regime.

My Eastern European childhood with its multi-cultural and vibrant Jewish community, such as I experienced in Sibiu, no longer exists. By 1980, the population of Sibiu had increased five-fold since my youth to 150,000, now nearly all Romanians. Tragically, the Holocaust decimated the Jewish populations of Eastern Europe. Today, the Sibiu synagogue remains a historic site, but no longer functions as a synagogue, because there is no Jewish community to sustain it.

The once thriving, dynamic, and cutting-edge cultural city of Vienna is now purely Austrian. It is a beautiful place, but the people and the community that I loved are gone. When the war was over and the Nazi atrocities were known, it turned out that no one in Austria had been a Nazi. But I know the truth. Whenever I visit Vienna, I am haunted by the clouds of the past, gazing at me with questioning eyes.[51]

A few years after the end of the war, we visited Vienna and met with Johanna and Joseph Kohel. Johanna was Gisy's childhood friend, who hid me in her home in my last few days in Vienna in June 1938. Johanna's husband Joseph had been a high-ranking Nazi official and had just recently returned from prison after a multi-year sentence for war crimes. At our get-together, both of them were remarkably friendly towards us, but Johanna shocked us when she made several positive comments about Hitler's regime. Gisy and I chose not to broach the subject of the Holocaust or the murder of six million Jews. Despite Johanna's reprehensible views, we will always be extremely grateful for her kindness. Johanna had proven to be a courageous and true friend. She had saved my life while putting herself and potentially her marriage at risk.

On another vacation, this time to Merano in Northern Italy, I met a German woman on the terrace of a coffeehouse. In the course of our conversation, I mentioned my personal story and the cruelty perpetrated by the Nazis. The German women said that she could not believe my account, but she kept on listening attentively. After I described my involvement in the tragic loss of 50 Jewish orphans, tears began to run down her face. She could hardly talk and in a choked voice, she said that she was ashamed to be a German. I suspect many Germans are reticent to deal with the demons of the past.

My family is beholden to those individuals who made our escape possible. Without the help of those strangers who risked their own lives, their family and their friends, we would never have survived. In our story, I give testament to the most charitable acts of kindness by Mme Roulet, the Ventre family, Mme Gamel, Monseigneur X, the "Drunk" Maquis, and the Spanish smuggler Manuel. They helped us as well as countless others flee from the Nazis.

I want to praise the Jewish relief agencies that were an indispensable resource and a beacon for good. The heroic efforts by the Quakers and the Unitarians saved the lives of men, women, and children of a different faith.

Many years have passed since our flight from Austria, and Gisy and I talk about these events often, marveling at the courage, daring, and initiative necessary for our escape. We were like hummingbirds at the top of a forest in flames. We moved with rapidly fluttering wings from one place to another, the flames always reaching but never touching us. We were lucky that we were always at the periphery of the conflagration.

I have lived over 80 years with more than half of those years in the United States. It is a long time, and I have tried my best to make the most of each moment. I encourage you to do the same.

---

51 "Vienna was destroyed—by Hitler to be sure, but also by itself. The image of howling Nazi mobs beating old Jews will not wash off history as easily as the political slogans Jews were forced to scrub off city walls with toothbrushes, no matter how much the Viennese proclaim their innocence and victimhood. For in the end, it was the Viennese themselves who opted for wealthy Prussian provincialism over cultural and intellectual excellence that might have restored the city's greatness. All that is left today are the monuments." Weyr, *The Setting of the Pearl: Vienna under Hitler*, xiii.

Austrians were disproportionately overrepresented among the Nazi's anti-Jewish terror organizations. While Austria represented only 8% of the German-speaking Empire, Austrians were 14% of SS members, 40% of the staff of several of the concentration camps, and 80% of Adolf Eichmann's Jewish Genocide staff. Of the pre-war Austrian Jewish population of 200,000, 65,000 were murdered and 135,000 successfully emigrated from Austria. The two largest Austrian banks acquired gold extracted from teeth removed from Jewish victims, directly from the concentration camps. Steininger, *Austria, Germany, and the Cold War: From the Anschluss to the State Treaty, 1938–1950*, 14–16.

My parents first told me about their Holocaust experience when I was in grammar school and too young to understand. The *Chicago Tribune* was scheduled to print an article about my parents and they didn't want my sister Sharon and me to hear about their stories from someone else. What I took away from their tale—and from other things my parents said and did—was that the world is a dangerous place and many people do bad things to other people, so do not trust anyone. Also, we should always be prepared for the next Holocaust. The way I pictured it was like the story of Little Red Riding Hood. There were evil people like the wolf who pretended to be the nice grandma. It took me a long time and many years of therapy to believe that there were also good people, like the huntsman who were brave and could outsmart the evil people.

In our daily life, my father never spoke about the war, but his feelings were expressed through his terrible nightmares. As a child, I heard his otherworldly screams, and my mother yelling, "Daddy, Daddy, wake up." My father's cries brought the terror into the present and contributed to my own PTSD.

My mother would sometimes tell stories to Sharon and me about the war (while braiding our hair before school), usually to scare us into behaving the way she wanted. For example, my mother would tell us what happened to my Aunt Clara. After the *Anschluss*, Clara's Aryan husband chose to stay in Austria and demanded a divorce. My interpretation of Clara's husband's betrayal was that you can't even trust your spouse.

Trusting people has always been a challenge for me. When I had my son, Danny, I was very concerned that my attitudes and behavior would negatively affect him. I did not want my son to grow up distrusting people too. I also didn't want to overprotect him as my parents had done with me. I went to a support group for children of Holocaust survivors, hoping to heal some of my angst that was spilling over into my relationship with my son. That survivor workshop did not help. The other members of the group were much worse off than I was, and they were trying to avoid jail, drug overdoses, nervous breakdowns, prostitution, and suicide. My own concerns about my son seemed minor in comparison. So I tried my best in my own way to protect him from the dangers of the world. His response has been to look danger in the eye, travel and work all over the world, make and keep friends everywhere, and take plenty of risks. He is a happy guy. Whew.

When I was a young girl, I told my mother that I wanted to be a ballerina and to move in with my Uncle Max's family in London to attend the school of the Sadler's Wells Ballet. My mother said that was not possible. She said that she and my father had survived the war so that their children could make a difference in the world, and ballet would not accomplish that. After these discussions, I considered becoming a research scientist and finding a cure for cancer, but my limited math abilities prevented that career choice. So I became a social worker specializing in private geriatric care management. It was a good choice and my parents were proud of my work. Interestingly, it is my son, working in developmental economics, focusing on combating hunger in third world countries, who is making a significant difference in the world.

Later in life, I found a man I could trust without reservations. My third husband, Wylie, is a wonderful role model of optimism, trust, good humor, and patience, as well as many other qualities that I cherish. Wylie always sees the glass as half full, and expects it to be full at any minute. His perspective has been a wonderful learning experience and made my life far more joyful.

I always loved to hear my Grandpa George recount tales of his miraculous escape from Europe. His stories were like a fast-paced action thriller with my grandparents and mother in the lead roles. They faced challenges and solved problems that many people face in wartime: finding food, seeking shelter, locating lost relatives in the turmoil, negotiating with an indifferent bureaucracy, and finding a way to make ends meet. All of Europe was in a state of crisis, but because my grandparents were Jewish, their daily life was especially hazardous. Unlike ordinary French civilians, my Jewish grandparents were actively hunted by the Nazis.

During their difficult and often frightening journey to freedom, my grandparents took substantial risks. In the war, very few Jews were successful in fleeing the Nazis' trap. In nearly every escape, the survivor's story is extraordinary, full of unexpected serendipitous twists and calamitous turns. The ordinary stories are untold because they did not survive.

In 1940, my grandmother gave birth prematurely to a son in Marseille. The death of this child was a great loss and caused my grandparents much grief, but if the baby had lived, I wonder if they would have been able or willing to take the dangerous trip over the Pyrenees with the Maquis.

My grandfather feared Hitler's anti-Semitism. He took the Nazi threat seriously, and he moved quickly and with great effort to emigrate from Austria and then France. He told me that if I sensed increasing persecution, hostility, and physical danger in my life, that I should be proactive, and relocate quickly. His escape had been narrow and precarious. Best to go early and return when the threat had subsided.

My grandfather encouraged me to go to medical school like he and my father had done, so that if I needed to flee from America, I would have the necessary skills to support my family in a foreign country. I told my grandfather that Jews were safe in America, but he replied that he had similar views when he was my age living in Vienna, and his assessments turned out to be wrong. So, I did my best to persuade my grandfather that a career in stock and bond trading was worthy, and that those skills were even more portable.

George was never completely reassured that his life in America was permanent. He kept a substantial sum in a non-interest bearing, numbered, Swiss bank account, and he encouraged me to do the same. He did this because he wanted to make sure that he would not have to start over again with no savings.

While my grandfather's concern for Jews living in America seems overstated, he would have been on target if I had been born and raised in a different country.

Prior to World War II, Jews had vibrant communities all over the world: in Europe, the United States, the USSR, and the Arab states. Today, world Jewry exists predominantly in just two places: the United States and Israel. Anti-Semitism did not end with the defeat of the Nazis. In the years after the Holocaust, 99% of my grandfather's fellow Romanian Jews emigrated. For example, as recently as the 1970s and 1980s, the former Romanian dictator, Ceaușescu, ransomed Jews still living in Romania to Israel for more than $2,000 per person and up to $25,000 for a doctor or scientist. Since 1989, 1.6 million out of the 1.9 million Jewish population from the former Soviet states have emigrated with over 1 million relocating to Israel.

In recent years, there have been increasingly common outbreaks of anti-Semitism in France. I wonder if my grandfather would advise French Jews to emigrate because of the recent incidents of violence against them. Or, would he be confident that this time the French civil service, police and judiciary would guarantee the civil liberties and physical safety of its Jewish citizens?

In 1989, my sister Debbie and I visited Vienna. We went to see the *Stadttempel* synagogue where my grandparents were married. The sanctuary was built in 1820 after the Austrian Emperor Joseph had made an edict that only Roman Catholic churches could have a public street façade, so the *Stadttempel* was hidden behind other residential and commercial buildings. During *Kristallnacht* in November 1938, most of the other synagogues in Vienna were torched, but *Stadttempel* was unscathed because the shul could not be burned down without destroying their neighbor's property. As a result, *Stadttempel* was the sole surviving Jewish place of worship after the war, while the other 93 synagogues in Vienna were destroyed. Today, the temple has very strict security, and when my sister and I entered the facility, the staff interrogated us, demanded to see our passports, and required us to pass through a metal detector. We later learned that eight years prior to our visit, Palestinian terrorists had used machine guns and a grenade to kill two and injure many more during a bar mitzvah ceremony at the temple.

When we returned home, my Great Aunt Inga mentioned that if there had been no Hitler, our family gatherings would have likely been in Vienna. My Great Uncle Emil disagreed. He said that he had faced significant anti-Semitism before Hitler, and he recalled that his grade school teacher had called him a Jewish pig. In 1936, two years before the *Anschluss*, Emil was arrested for his active participation in the Austrian Social Democratic Workers Party, and subsequently moved from Vienna to Paris. I told Emil that I was extremely impressed by Viennese architecture; even the central police station was beautiful. Emil replied that many of his best friends had been tortured in the basement of that very same building.

My grandfather loved growing up in Sibiu, Romania, but he was enamored with German culture, so he relocated to Vienna to enjoy German theater, literature, and the arts while attending graduate school at Austria's best university. When he met Gisy, what he found attractive about her was not just her natural beauty, but also her melodious German accent, and her ability to quote extended passages from Schiller and Goethe. The anti-Semitism that my grandfather experienced in Vienna in 1938 was for George a personal betrayal.

After the war, Vienna was decimated, no longer the cultural mecca of George's youth or a center for creativity in music (Mahler), painting (Klimt), furniture, ceramics, glass, and textiles (Hoffmann and Moser). Vienna never regained its leadership in psychology, medicine, or the sciences.

For my grandparents, like most Austrian émigrés, returning to live in Austria after the war was not considered as an option. They were too traumatized and angered by their Austrian wartime experiences and preferred to make a new life in the United States.

From time to time, my grandparents did go back to visit the old country. On those trips, they would visit their favorite restaurants and cultural sites, and meet with their old acquaintances. Some of these relationships improved because of the war, and others were strained or severed. Gisy was very close with her neighbor in Chelles who had agreed to store Gisy's personal belongings when she was forced to evacuate. After the war, the neighbor told Gisy that all of her possessions had been confiscated or lost. Some years later, Gisy and Susie traveled to France and visited her. Gisy's personal belongings were visibly displayed in her home, including hand towels with Gisy's monogrammed initials. She never spoke to this friend ever again.

On another trip—described in my grandfather's memoir—my grandparents went to visit the Kohels in their Viennese home just after the war. Johanna was joined by her husband Joseph who had recently been released from prison after serving a sentence for war crimes. In the discussion, Johanna praised Hitler, but my grandparents chose not to engage. I assume they did not debate the virtues of the Nazi regime because there was little to gain.

Johanna had hidden my grandfather when he feared that he might be arrested by the Gestapo. My grandparents were both very thankful for Johanna's courage and friendship, and her efforts probably saved their lives. Yet, the meeting also reveals the complexity of human relationships. I suspect that Johanna did not inform her husband at the time of George's presence in their house, as Joseph was then a high-ranking Nazi official away on important government business. I am sure he would have disapproved for many reasons, including the risk that if George was found to be hiding in his house, his career would be jeopardized. I wonder when Johanna told her husband about this ruse. Was it during the war or afterwards? Maybe she told him during his plea bargain negotiations for his war crimes, to give evidence that he had actively tried to help Jews? Or, did she tell him moments before my grandparents arrived at the house?

I wonder what kind of cognitive dissonance is necessary to love and to remain married to someone who has committed a war crime. Is it easier under the circumstances to believe in the good things that Hitler accomplished and to deny the genocide? Did Johanna make these pro-Hitler comments at their get-together for my grandparent's benefit or was she trying to reassure her husband that she remained his ally? We will never know. But, we do know that people are complicated. Most people would have looked the other way in my grandfather's moment of need, but Johanna did not. Whether she was motivated to help my grandfather because she was Gisy's lifelong friend, or because she knew it was the right thing to do, it does not matter. She saved a life and for that I will always be indebted.

I wonder what I would have done under the circumstances, living in wartime Vichy France. If I were a Jew, I would certainly be on the run, but if not it seems unlikely that I would have lived up in the hills, with a revolver at my side, helping refugees cross the mountains.

I would like to think I would join the French Resistance in some capacity but most Vichy French citizens did not. My hope is that I would not fall into the trap of indifference. I think one of the most important lessons of my grandfather's experience is that sometimes you must disobey the laws of the state to preserve your own and your nation's deepest values.

I find my grandfather's perspective to be surprisingly non-judgmental. In contrast, my grandmother never forgave the Germans. She was angry and justifiably so. There would be no German-made items in her home. The sole exception was Grandpa's Mercedes that was parked in the attached garage.

George lived to be 85 years old and died in 1987, and despite announcing that she planned to live to 100, Gisy passed away at 97 in 2006. As their grandson, I had the pleasure of enjoying both of them for many years and benefited greatly from their wisdom, love, and affection.

—Larry Bernstein, son of Susan and Ira

When my dad retired at 80 from his medical practice, he decided to write his memoirs so that his children and grandchildren would know their family's story. His first undertaking was to learn how to type. Once he mastered that skill, he proceeded to type for several hours daily until he completed his memoirs.

I was amazed at his recall of dates, names, locations, events and small details. Reading his drafts was emotionally difficult for me as I remembered many of the events as well as others he did not include. I recalled being upset when my fellow classmates at the Catholic school in Marseille called me the "farmer's child." It was confusing to pretend to be someone I was not.

Even though I was young, only five-years-old, I remember rushing into the bomb shelters at night, being hungry, and never having any playmates. But I was comforted that I was always near my mother and often with both of my parents.

Yes, I remember climbing the Pyrenees at night and hiding in caves during the day. I was very cold, especially when I got wet. The steep climbs were particularly difficult. Above all, I was most afraid of making too much noise, which would put everyone else at risk. After a while, being quiet, alert, careful, and on guard became second nature to me. What surprises me now is that a five year old could keep still and behave in the desired manner. Undoubtedly, our previous years of hiding, being constantly hungry, and on-the-run prepared me for such an arduous and frightening journey.

When we arrived in Lisbon, I remember a Portuguese family who helped us while we were waiting for a ship to take us to the United States. They had a sweet, small dog that I would play with for hours. It was the first time in my life that I was not running or hiding. I suspect that my love for dogs began because of this positive connection.

The voyage aboard the *Serpa Pinto* to the United States was very enjoyable for me. I loved being free and was full of anticipation for my new life. I neither suffered from seasickness nor worried about the future like my parents. I was overjoyed.

Once we arrived in the U.S., I made the decision to communicate only in English. No one should speak to me in French or German anymore! In retrospect, this was a mixed blessing. My family and I managed to learn English quickly which was great, but much later I regretted losing my fluency in French and German.

As astonishing as our escape was, I am also impressed that my parents enthusiastically pursued a new life in America. They did not dwell on the past and were not deterred by the many obstacles. Dad learned a new language, studied, and passed medical examinations and worked in a required, unpaid, year-long medical internship program.

When my dad opened his medical practice, my mom worked in the office full-time as his nurse, secretary, and receptionist. Luckily, I did not always have to go home to an empty apartment because my Aunt Sophie and Uncle Bill lived in the same building. When I visited Sophie, she taught me how to bake and cook. None of my school friends' mothers worked, so I felt different.

My parents worked hard, long hours, but never complained. In addition to his private practice, my dad also worked as a physician for the Chicago Public schools as well as for a union. My father used to tell me that America was the Promised Land; in no country are there opportunities for those willing to work and to succeed as in America. My mom and dad were intent on remaking our lives as Americans and to live the American Dream. At the earliest possible opportunity, we all became American citizens.

A few years later, my two sisters, Erica and Sharon, were born, and we were now a happy family of five. I felt like a second mom as I was 12 and 13 years older than my two sisters. I babysat and did the grocery shopping and helped with food preparation, which was very satisfying, and a great learning experience.

I did not speak to others about my wartime experiences, because I wanted to move forward with my life. As a child, I just wanted to fit in, speak English without an accent and be accepted.

In the back of my mind, I have always questioned why? Why were people trying to kill me? After all I was just a five-year-old child? Why did so many of our family members and friends have to die? Why did the Nazis kill millions of innocent people? I could not understand how a civilized society could become so filled with hate that they would dedicate themselves to exterminating the Jews? Why would the Germans use their limited resources during the war for a genocide project? It isn't easy to kill millions of people. Tens of thousands of workers were required to build and run the concentration camps. A substantial bureaucracy was needed to make the necessary plans and manage the logistics. Architects designed camps, engineers built structures, chemists manufactured poisons, bankers financed projects, and police and soldiers sought out individuals in hiding. For example, the Marseille roundup of Jews on January 23, 1943, required 10,000 French policemen sent from all over southern France. So many people needed to be complicit. Where was the disgust? Where was the public and private outcry? Where was the press? How could this not be stopped? The post-war argument of just following orders is nonsense. No one forced the locksmiths to open the doors in the wee hours on that frightful morning in Marseille, or put a gun to the train conductor to haul the cattle cars full of innocent civilians to the concentration camps. How could modern cultured societies be responsible for causing such a catastrophe?

All my life I have tried to understand this cruel, sadistic, and often indifferent behavior, but I cannot make sense of it. Tragically, the world over, man's inhumanity to other men continues.

My sisters say they were harmed by my family's traumatic wartime experiences, but I was not. In fact, I feel just the opposite. Our escape made me stronger and better able to handle adversity. I am a problem-solver and try to be as self-reliant as possible.

I have survivor's guilt. I enjoy my marriage, happy children, and career, but it never seems to be enough to justify why I survived and others did not. I think about it often but I do not dwell on these questions because there is likely no answer.

I would like to conclude with a passage from my father's original edition of this book.

Our good fortune to escape the massive destruction of our people was due to the unexpected help of many people we did not even know. There were, and we hope there will always be, heroes of this type—heroes for whom odes are never written; heroes who did not deserve this title because of feats performed on battlefields but for deeds done in self-sacrifice, in risk of their own lives with courage and nobility of purpose.

This book is dedicated to those individuals who helped in those critical times, most of whose names were not even known to us—others whose names were forgotten. Only a few are remembered by name. However, we give our gratitude to all of them.

Honor those who make sacrifices to save a child.

For those interested in additional reading on this subject I would suggest any of the following:

Man's Search for Meaning. Viktor Frankl's book is about survival in concentration camps and explores Nietzsche's quote: "He who has a Why to live for can bear almost any How."

Surrender on Demand. Varian Fry's describes his efforts to save European intellectuals and artists from the Nazis in Vichy France in 1940-1941.

Vichy France and the Jews. Michael Marrus and Robert Paxton explore the complicity of the Vichy French civilian leadership in the massacre of French Jews. The book details the anti-Semitic legislation that was critical to the roundup of the Jews in France. In addition, they provide additional information about the Quaker mission to save 50 Jewish children who were supposed to travel with my grandparents on the *Serpa Pinto*.

The Holocaust and the Jews of Marseille—The Enforcement of Anti-Semitic Policies in Vichy France. Donna Ryan depicts life in Marseille before the occupation as well as the round-up of the Jews after the Gestapo takes control of the city in January 1943.

The Devil in France—My Encounter with Him in the Summer of 1940. Lion Feuchtwanger, a famous German-Jewish writer and Nazi critic, was interned with my grandfather in Nîmes. He reports what it was like to live in the camp and criticizes the French bureaucracy's indifference to the plight of Jewish refugees.

In Rescue Flight: American Relief Workers Who Defied the Nazis. Susan Subak describes the relief agencies' activities in wartime France and the important role of René Zimmer, who was my grandfather's immediate supervisor at the Marseille medical clinic. The book also profiles Danny Bénédite, who was employed by Varian Fry, and his later clandestine work with the Maquis and the OSS.

Rescuing the Children: A Holocaust Memoir. Vivette Samuel tells how the Jewish Children's Aid Society placed Jewish children with foster parents. Vivette's husband Julian worked with my grandfather at the Marseille medical clinic.

Suite Française a novel. Irène Némirovsky tells the story of a French wife of a prisoner of war who falls in love with a German officer during the occupation.

A Song for You by Sharon Karp. Please watch my Aunt Sharon's film *A Song for You,* co-directed by Silvia Malagrino, which gives a different perspective of my grandparents' escape. The film has interviews with Gisy and her three daughters: Sharon, Susan, and Erica, as they travel across France and Spain following their parents' escape route. In the film, they describe how their parents' traumatic experience continues to affect their lives. A DVD of the film is available at http://asongforyoumovie.com.

Shoah by Claude Lanzmann is a riveting 9-hour documentary on the Holocaust with interviews with former Nazis and victims.

The Sorrow and the Pity by Marcel Ophüls is a 4-hour documentary on Vichy France and how the French collaborated with the Germans.

Watermarks is a documentary by Yaron Zilberman about the pre-war Vienna sports club Hakoah. My grandma Gisy was a member of this Jewish sports club.

Woman in Gold, starring Helen Mirren chronicles a Jewish woman's struggle to retrieve Klimt's most famous painting—of her aunt Adele Bloch-Bauer—which had been stolen from her family by the Nazis.

Life is Beautiful is an Italian comedy about a father and son imprisoned together in a concentration camp.

Schindler's List won the academy award for best picture and is directed by Steven Spielberg. The film portrays Oskar Schindler's efforts to save his Jewish employees during the Holocaust.

A SONG FOR YOU

A Film by **SHARON KARP** *Co-Directed by* **SILVIA MALAGRINO**

In 1943, the Karp family escaped the Nazis by crossing the Pyrenees on foot with the help of the French Resistance. For five harrowing years, they were on the run, sometimes only steps ahead of Hitler's troops.

Carrying the burden of their parent's trauma, the filmmaker and her sisters return to Europe to confront events of the past in an attempt to separate them from the present.

The story is told through interviews with her mother, segments of a book her father wrote, home movies, photographs, documents and historical footage. The mother's songs are threaded throughout the film. Singing brought relief and hope in desperate times.

A Song for You is a story of survival through strength of will, luck, and the help of others.

The film opened in January, 2014 at the Gene Siskel Center in Chicago, and is being shown across the country. *A Song for You* is now available for screenings in universities, colleges, high schools, libraries and other institutions on DVD, BluRay and digital download. To schedule a screening, please visit the film's website, asongforyoumovie.com.